MW00812205

ANCIENT
ROOTS AND RUINS

A Guide to Understanding the Romans,
Their World, and Their Language

Grades 4–8

ANCIENT
ROOTS AND RUINS

A Guide to Understanding the Romans, Their World, and Their Language

Ariel Baska and Joyce VanTassel-Baska, Ed.D.

PRUFROCK PRESS INC.
WACO, TEXAS

ACKNOWLEDGMENTS

To my current, former, and future Latin students for everything they teach me every day. —Ariel Baska

To my former Latin professor Frederick Wheelock for instilling in me the joy and love of the Latin language and its heritage. —Joyce VanTassel-Baska

Library of Congress Cataloging-in-Publication Data

Baska, Ariel.
  Ancient roots and ruins : a guide to understanding the Romans, their world, and their language
/ by Ariel Baska and Joyce VanTassel-Baska, Ed.D.
      pages cm.
  ISBN 978-1-61821-091-3 (pbk.)
  1. Rome--Civilization. 2. Rome--Antiquities. 3. Rome--Social life and customs. 4. Latin
language--History. I. Title.
  DG77.B37 2013
  937--dc23
                            2013020348

Copyright © 2014 Prufrock Press Inc.

Edited by Bethany Johnsen

Cover and layout design by Raquel Trevino

ISBN-13: 978-1-61821-091-3

No part of this book may be reproduced, translated, stored in a retrieval system, or transmitted,
in any form or by any means, electronic, mechanical, photocopying, microfilming, recording, or
otherwise, without written permission from the publisher.

Prufrock Press grants the individual purchasing this book permission to photocopy original
activity pages for single classroom use. This permission does not include electronic reproduction
rights. Should you wish to make copies of materials we sourced or licensed from others, request
permission from the original publisher before reproducing that material.

For more information about our copyright policy or to request reprint permissions, visit http://
www.prufrock.com/permissions.

Printed in the United States of America.

At the time of this book's publication, all facts and figures cited are the most current available.
All telephone numbers, addresses, and website URLs are accurate and active. All publications,
organizations, websites, and other resources exist as described in the book, and all have been
verified. The authors and Prufrock Press Inc. make no warranty or guarantee concerning the
information and materials given out by organizations or content found at websites, and we are
not responsible for any changes that occur after this book's publication. If you find an error, please
contact Prufrock Press Inc.

Prufrock Press Inc.
P.O. Box 8813
Waco, TX 76714-8813
Phone: (800) 998-2208
Fax: (800) 240-0333
http://www.prufrock.com

TABLE OF CONTENTS

PART I
BACKGROUND READINGS

CHAPTER 1

FROM THE BEGINNING (AB INITIO)

> *Carpe diem, quam minimum credula postero.*
> Seize the day, trust as little as possible in tomorrow.
>
> —Horace

This book is written for the purpose of understanding and reviving in a new generation of students an interest in the most important influence on Western civilization and especially Western Europe and the United States—the Latin language and the people who spoke it, the deeds they performed, and the inventions they created. We are indebted to the Romans for our legal system, our own language, our approaches to creating literature and the arts, and our very lifestyle today.

The audience for this book is students who are gifted and range in age from 9–14. It is written to introduce some of the most important ideas from the ancient Romans, as well as their history and their contributions to our current culture.

The book is intended for use as a core or supplementary text by English teachers at the middle school level, who may teach from it for a 9-week period. It may be used by elementary gifted teachers in cluster classrooms, or pull-out programs, as well as self-contained settings to augment the study of language and literature. As such, it may be taught for 6–9 weeks or interspersed throughout a semester.

This book may also be a good supplementary tool in a Latin I classroom, regardless of the age of the student, in order to provide a basic guide to many facets of Roman culture in English.

ORGANIZATION OF THE BOOK

The book is organized into two sections. Part I provides the background to understanding the Latin language in the context of history, art, literature, and linguistics, as well as providing specific examples of Latin vocabulary and grammar for students to study and learn.

Part II of the book provides students the opportunity to understand Roman culture through the study of important concepts—time, space, power, innovation, and expression. Each unit is organized around a set of key generalizations related to the concept, provides activities and resources for further exploration of the concept, and describes the way the idea has shaped Roman thought and action. Each unit also features important mythological and historical figures and their contributions to the ideas presented.

GIFTED LEARNERS AND THEIR NEEDS

> *Nullum saeculum magnis ingeniis clausum est.*
> No generation is closed to great talents.
>
> —Seneca

The book is conceptualized as a curriculum for gifted students, who can benefit at an early age from learning about the past through selected artifacts of an important culture and making the connections between our culture and the Romans', our language and theirs. The study of Latin responds to several characteristics and needs of gifted learners:

- **The gifted have advanced vocabularies and love to learn new words and phrases.** Latin provides the opportunity to learn many new words that are directly correlated to English words.

Even more common are the roots and stems of Latin words that may be found in the majority of English words, thus enhancing English vocabulary fourfold or more.

- **The gifted have inquisitive minds and curiosity about the origin of things.** The study of Latin enhances one's understanding of the history of Western Civilization and therefore of where we came from. Latin culture is suggested by many of our societal structures today and in the many artifacts left behind by the Romans all over the world, but particularly in Italy, Greece, Turkey, France, Britain, and all over the Middle East.

- **The gifted have complex thinking abilities that are enhanced by good memory.** Gifted learners can enjoy the complexities of the study of a language that has many characteristics like ours but also is more complex in its grammatical structure and forms. Vocabulary study can yield many new words and insights about language that should delight and astound them. They may also enjoy learning about the lives of famous Romans who reached intellectual heights that have not been surpassed and seeing them as role models for behavior and habits of mind.

- **The gifted have the capacity to make connections among diverse ideas.** This trait in the gifted is best nurtured by the access to ideas from multiple disciplines that allow connections to be made as a result. The book is organized by major concepts allowing students to make connections to the present day and to other periods of history, as these concepts have been vital over time.

- **The gifted love to create and invent anything, from imaginary friends to new objects created from scraps.** Because the gifted are creative, they will learn to appreciate deeply the Romans' capacity for building and creating structures in new forms and modes. In the book, students will have the opportunity to replicate many of these in their own projects.

DIFFERENTIATION OF CURRICULUM: THE INTEGRATED CURRICULUM MODEL (ICM)

The Integrated Curriculum Model (ICM) was first proposed in 1986, based on a review of the research literature on what worked with gifted learners, and further expounded upon in subsequent publications (VanTassel-Baska, 1986, 1998; VanTassel-Baska & Little, 2011). The model is comprised of three interrelated dimensions that are responsive to different aspects of the gifted learner:

1. *Emphasizing advanced content knowledge that frames disciplines of study.* Honoring the talent search concept, this facet of the model ensures that careful diagnostic-prescriptive approaches are employed to enhance the challenge level of the curriculum base. Curricula based on the model would represent advanced learning in any given discipline.

2. *Providing higher order thinking and processing.* This facet of the model promotes student opportunities for manipulating information at complex levels by employing generic thinking models like Paul's Elements of Reasoning (Paul & Elder, 2001) and more discipline-specific models like Sher's Nature of the Scientific Process (Sher, 1993). This facet of the ICM also promotes the utilization of information in generative ways, through project work and/or fruitful discussions.

3. *Organizing learning experiences around major issues, themes, and ideas that define understanding of a discipline and provide connections across disciplines.* This facet of the ICM scaffolds curricula for gifted learners around the important aspects of a discipline and emphasizes these aspects in a systemic way (Ward, 1981). Thus, themes and ideas are selected based on careful research of the primary area of study to determine the most worthy and important ideas for curriculum development, a theme consistent with reform curriculum specifications in key areas (American Association for the Advancement of Science, 1990; Perkins, 1992). The goal of such an approach is to ensure deep understanding of disciplines, rather than misconceptions.

These three relatively distinct curriculum dimensions have proven successful with gifted populations at various stages of development

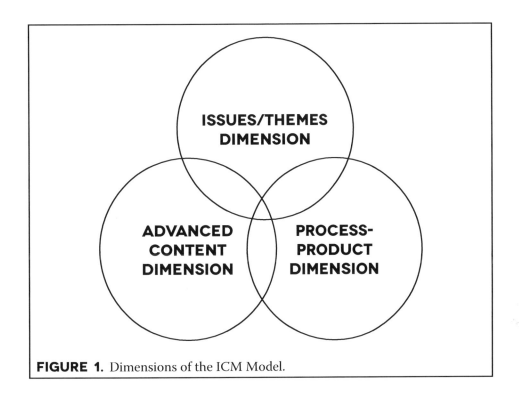

FIGURE 1. Dimensions of the ICM Model.

and in various domain-specific areas. Taken together, these research-based approaches formed the basis of the Integrated Curriculum Model (VanTassel-Baska, 1986a; VanTassel-Baska, 1998; VanTassel-Baska & Little, 2011; VanTassel-Baska & Stambaugh, 2006). Figure 1 portrays the interrelated dimensions of the ICM model just described.

Recent reviews of curricular interventions for the gifted have found the greatest effectiveness prevailing in an accelerative approach, guided by the content modification features exemplified in the ICM (Johnsen, 2000; VanTassel-Baska & Brown, 2007). The fusion of these approaches is central to the development of a coherent curriculum that is responsive to diverse needs of talented students while also providing rich challenges to all for optimal learning.

APPLICATION

Current work in the ICM model for the gifted has continued to focus on a merger with the curriculum reform principles advocating world-class standards in all traditional curricular areas (VanTassel-Baska & Little, 2011). The major shift in thinking regarding this orientation is from one that looks only at the optimal match between characteristics of the learner and the curriculum to a model based on performance in various domains, thereby letting the level of functioning determine who is ready for more advanced work in an area rather than a predictive measure. Thus, differentiation for any population is grounded in differential standards of performance at a given period of time. Standards are constant; time is the variable. Such an approach holds promise for gifted students in that the level and pace of curriculum *can* be adapted to their needs, and the existing state standards call for the kind of focus that curriculum writers for gifted students have long advocated—higher level thinking, interdisciplinary approaches, and an emphasis on student-centered learning.

Gifted students need high but realizable expectations for learning at each stage of development. Other students can also benefit from working to attain such standards. By the same token, gifted students can also benefit from a developmental and personal perspective on fostering their abilities at a close-up level, an emphasis requiring organizational models such as tutorials, mentorships, and small clusters to support it.

The Integrated Curriculum Model has been tested substantially in the areas of science and language arts in particular, using quasi-experimental research designs that compared pretest–posttest performance of students participating in the Center for Gifted Education units in these areas with the performance of similar students who were not taught using the units. The presentation of claims for student learning in each area have been substantiated by both quantitative and qualitative studies, demonstrating specifically the results related to the specific curriculum, as well as supporting the power of teaching concepts, higher level thinking, and advanced content to the gifted learner across stages of development.

Examples of curriculum and instructional modifications using the ICM. The examples provided in Table 1 illustrate the major dimensions of the ICM and the translation of those dimensions into differentiated approaches in each major content domain. The examples demonstrate the ways in which accelerated learning is promoted, the ways in which the higher level processes of thinking, problem solving and research are exploited, the types of generative products that students create, and the conceptual foundation for given units of study. These dimensions then may frame units of study for each area of learning, with varying units by grade level that typically cut across multiple grade level use. The shorthand table descriptions also suggest the nature of instructional approaches employed. Some examples are pulled from the unit here on the study of Latin.

TABLE 1

The Integrated Curriculum Model by Subject Area and Dimensions of Sample Unit Study

Content Area/Topic	Accelerative Approaches	Higher Level Thinking/ Problem-Solving	Product Tasks	Concept Theme
Science/ Innovation	Pretesting and compacting the study of Roman innovation	Reasoning model, scientific investigation skills, questions	Logs, experimental designs, problem-based learning (PBL) resolution project and presentation	Systems: Understanding the elements, boundaries, interactions, inputs and outputs of cells, plants, and terrariums
Language Arts	Reading selections based on ancient authors and calibrated two grade levels above	Reasoning model, literature web, persuasive writing, research project	Study of famous Romans through biography; with talent development markers	Change: The ways that change is everywhere, related to time, caused by people or nature, etc.
Mathematics	Advanced math skills in graphing, statistics, and estimation	Problem-based learning	Problem resolution in oral and written form for a real-world audience	Models that are conceptual and physical applied to understand phenomena
Social Studies	Emphasis on the systems of ancient civilizations that made them great	Emphasis on historical analysis, document study, and trends	Research on historical issues	Patterns of change over time as chronicled by historical events within and across cultures

The major approach to teaching the gifted must involve the use of differentiated curriculum. The ICM provides an effective way of using a research-based model for the organization of a unit of study. It is especially effective for this unit as it integrates the disciplines of study through the use of a central concept, organizes higher level thinking and problem solving through the use of questions and activities and projects, and uses the teaching of the Latin language, more typically taught at high school level, with younger students.

ALIGNMENT TO THE NAGC PROGRAM STANDARDS FOR THE GIFTED

This guidebook and the study of Latin itself aligns well to the learning and development, curriculum, learning environment, programming, and assessment standards of the new NAGC Gifted Programming Standards. Table 2 delineates the relationship of these standards to the corresponding aspect of the study of Latin as it is developed in this book.

WHY STUDY LATIN?

> He studied Latin like the violin, because he liked it.
> —Robert Frost

While the American Council on the Teaching of Foreign Languages (Draper & Hicks, 2002) reported that only 1.3% of high school students currently take Latin, the College Board, which administers the Advanced Placement program, reported a 95% increase since 1993 in students taking the Latin exam for college credit. States like Virginia, for example, offer Latin for gifted middle school students in selected school districts, run a statewide summer program in a rural area of the state, and offer it as a regular option for elementary students at college Saturday programs. Moreover, each year the state sponsors a 3-week Latin Academy in which selected students have the opportunity to immerse themselves in the subject with classics professors from across the state. What has caused such a resurgence of interest in a subject frequently made fun of for its irrelevance? Perhaps the new American obsession with standards

TABLE 2
NAGC Program Standards Met by This Book

Standard	How It's Met
Standard 1: Learning and Development	• Self-Understanding: Students reflect on their own cultural identity in their study of ancient ways, considering their own beliefs, traditions, and values. • Cognitive and Affective Growth: Students learn about the complexities of language and linguistic structure that can provide a worthwhile challenge for our brightest students.
Standard 2: Assessment	• Learning Progress/Outcomes: Gifted students can complete meaningful assessments more easily in an elective class not burdened with high stakes testing. The cumulative nature of learning a second language makes formative assessments more meaningful to chart progress through language ability.
Standard 3: Curriculum Planning and Instruction	• Curriculum Planning: Latin is not a spoken language, which puts less pressure on English as a Second Language (ESL) students. It is an ideal language for students from disadvantaged backgrounds and twice-exceptional students. Latin also improves study skills and gives students with weaknesses in language arts a "formula" for the way that language works. • Talent Development: Students with various areas of interest and talent can excel in Latin, due to its extraordinarily interdisciplinary quality • Culturally Relevant Curriculum: Latin curriculum is rooted in Roman culture, drawing constant comparison to various ways of life, both in the U.S. and around the world. In a multicultural and diverse society, a language that is currently taught in 112 different countries on every continent gives students an entrée to the global market. Where dialects in modern languages change over time and in different places, Latin learners in China, Berlin, and Belize all speak the same language.
Standard 4: Learning Environments	• Communications Competence: Students must demonstrate oral and written skills in the Latin classroom, where there is a strong emphasis on different modes of communication, not just speaking, the focus of most world language classrooms. • Cultural Competence: Most standard Latin curriculum includes a study of various Roman systems, and the comparison between the American system versus the Roman system and the revelations about each culture as a result.
Standard 5: Programming	• Variety of Programming: Latin is a powerful elective course that demonstrates a commitment to giving students choice in their education. • Collaboration: Students benefit from the interdisciplinary nature of Latin, and the way it promotes understanding of history, the arts, and culture. Teachers may collaborate across departments to make the course of study even more relevant for students.

and substantive learning may have helped bring about the trend. Critics would contend that (1) Latin is a "dead" language with no practical value; (2) it does not "train" the mind as once believed; (3) it is difficult; (4) it is text-based learning, not aural-oral in technique; and (5) it is irrelevant to today's youth. Nevertheless, many educators and students have found it to be useful in many ways.

Latin has many hidden benefits that are not often explicated and, therefore, are not well-understood. It is especially well-matched to verbally precocious learners who have the capacity to handle abstraction and rigorous analytical activity. The following benefits are worthy of commentary:

1. Latin develops intellectual habits of mind. It provides a structure for thinking about language that can be transferred to other work as well. Studies have shown its positive impact on minority student learning in reading and mathematics, for example (Harrington-Lueker, 1992).

2. Latin teaches deep analysis. It forces students to think deeply about what they are learning. Analyzing complex sentence structures and word forms focuses attention on the interplay of form and substance. Because a student must "work" in Latin, success at unlocking translations yields deeper understanding of these language forms and the ideas they present about antiquity.

3. Latin provides an understanding of Western heritage. How do mainstream U.S. students understand their roots? One wonderful strategy is to learn Latin, the language of Western thought and civilization. Reading ancient writers and thinkers provides an understanding of contemporary ideas.

4. Latin enhances English vocabulary. One year of Latin benefits students significantly in enhancing English vocabulary learning, even in comparison to students taking a Greek and Latin roots course in English (VanTassel-Baska, 1987). Other studies have shown enhanced reading ability for students who have taken Latin for only one year over students who have taken 4 years in other languages (Van Stekelenburg, 1984).

5. Latin enhances English linguistic competency. Because students must learn the rudiments of English grammar in order to master Latin forms, they become more familiar with their own language. As a consequence, they also show enhanced understanding of English grammar after only a year of Latin learning (Van Tassel-Baska, 1987).

6. Latin provides a strong base for third language learning. Because so many languages are derived from Latin, typical school languages like French and Spanish are made easier for students to acquire after a year or two of Latin (Prager, 2000).

7. Latin exemplifies interdisciplinary studies by combining history, literature, art, and philosophy with the study of the language itself. If educators want to enhance interdisciplinary learning, teaching Latin is an ideal way to do it. Studying a language penetrates the heart of a culture as no other approach does other than living in the culture itself. Language conveys all of the symbols, ideas, and relevant cues about a culture to an outsider, making it easier to understand.

8. Latin provides the challenge of learning a new abstract symbol system. Learning Latin provides a slake for the thirst of gifted students for challenge. It is complex, yet logical, systematic, and yields enjoyment through opportunities to study classical literature and ancient history. Both public and private schools have found that Latin learning enlivens elementary classrooms (Wilhelm & Wilhelm, 1991).

9. Latin provides higher level thinking through constant analogies from contemporary ideas to Roman and Greek thought. Latin engages students in higher level thought with proverbs, idioms, and commentary from eminent authors. It provides them with the basic philosophical tenets of life; thus, Latin might be regarded as "Confucianism for Westerners." Its authors explicate both the Stoic and Epicurean philosophies, ways of being in the world still seen today as archetypes for living.

LATIN AS AN ACCELERATIVE EXPERIENCE

Only two subjects are comparatively easy to accelerate in our schools at any level: mathematics and foreign language. The reason for this is their cumulative organizational patterns, where incrementalization is essential to learning the subjects deeply and well. Thus, Latin offers a special opportunity to accelerate learning for gifted students. It may begin as early as fifth grade and be formally taught from then on. Proficiency in the first 2 years of high school may be attained by most gifted students by the end of their eighth-grade year. Advanced Placement (AP) options may be accessed by the sophomore and junior years in high school. Because

TABLE 3
Acceleration of Latin Study—Student A

Grade 5	Introduction to Latin in elementary workbooks during the summer
Grade 6	Study of Cambridge Latin series; learning of forms, vocabulary, and translation
Grade 7	Complete study of Latin I material with proficiency test through homeschooling
Grade 8	Latin II (Caesar) in high school classroom
Grade 9	Latin III (Cicero) in high school classroom
Grade 10	Latin IV AP (Vergil's Aeneid) in high school classroom; College French in summer
Grade 11	Latin V AP (Catullus and Horace) on independent study; high school French III and IV on 4x4 block schedule; attended Summer Language Latin Academy
Grade 12	College French (2 semesters)

of logical organizational patterns and a tight scope and sequence, acceleration of the subject is made easier to accomplish through use of a diagnostic-prescriptive technique.

Table 3 depicts one student's accelerative experience in Latin, beginning in the fifth grade and culminating in advanced work in a second language as well. Acceleration within a Latin course can also occur with regularity for gifted learners. The basic grammatical structures of gender, number, and case can be compressed and used as a basis for "prescribing" learning, with careful follow-up assessment. Practice in constructions and other grammatical experiences can be truncated for the gifted while all vocabulary and most translations should be learned for building competency and cultural value. Studies from talent search universities have continued to demonstrate that a year of Latin can be compressed into 75 hours of instruction in the summer while retaining strong mastery over time (VanTassel-Baska & Olszewski-Kubilius,1988). During the academic year, accelerating the pace of learning by grouping gifted learners together in the Latin classroom has also been found to be effective (Coffin, 1981). New online materials in Latin also allow for greater self-pacing in learning the language (McManus, 2001) and alternative roles for Latin teachers as facilitators of language learning (Shelton, 2000).

Student A went on to study the classics in college as her major and became a Latin teacher at the high school level, teaching all years up through Advanced Placement.

LEARNING OUTCOMES FROM LATIN INSTRUCTION

What specific learning do students accrue from taking Latin? The following sets of learning clusters are examples of the types of outcomes students can achieve (VanTassel-Baska, 2004). Latin is a route to understanding word relationships. Students come to understand English roots, stems, and cognates that come from Latin. Because 60% of our words are derived from Latin, it provides an important and economical vocabulary development tool. Moreover, synonyms, antonyms, and homonyms become more interesting as students learn more Latin-derived English words. Learning how to construct analogies and how to understand them also becomes a part of the basic word relationship model that Latin offers. Latin is also a route to understanding linguistics, the grammar and syntax of language, its sentence patterns, and its underlying units of meaning. Because much of learning Latin is grounded in syntactical construction, students become highly sensitized to the structure of language and the constant comparison of English and Latin in this dimension. Latin is a route to creative production. Students can take Latin out of its context and apply it to contemporary life. Linkages to applied fields like architecture, engineering, and athletics may be made, showing how the underpinning of each field owes its basic structure to the Romans. Creative activities may include the following:
- performing the ancient plays of Plautus and Terence;
- translating English favorites like *Winnie the Pooh* into Latin;
- analyzing the rise and fall of the Roman Empire in relationship to more contemporary empires like Great Britain and the U.S.;
- conducting a study of Roman dress by creating costumes and holding a fashion show;
- designing logos using Latin sayings and idioms; and
- creating modern analogues of Roman myths.

Latin provides a direct route to understanding modern democratic governments. Cicero's ideas are as timely today as they were in first-century Rome. His concern for the rule of law, representational democracy, and the people's will to have avenues of expression are all contained in his writings. His and other Romans' ideas still govern our lives through the constitutions of both the United States and Great Britain (Everitt, 2001). Modern politics can be understood through the formation of ancient coalitions like the triumvirates, which were made up of men who each had something important to contribute, but could only gain power through collaborating with others. The seeds of special interest groups were sown in Roman politics, as well as the spirit of oratory in moving people to action, swaying opinion, and ultimately deciding the fate of individuals and groups.

Latin can also play a large part in personal relevance and creating meaning. Many universal ideas of philosophy over the centuries can be traced back to Greek and Roman roots. Two major ancient philosophies, Epicureanism and Stoicism, frame our current views of how to lead a good life. Does human happiness lie in mastering our strong emotions and ordering our desires in accordance with moral duty, as the Stoic school argued, or in accepting that there is no afterlife for our souls and pursuing pleasure and freedom from pain, along with the Epicureans? The Romans asked themselves these questions, even as we do today. Other central themes explored in a study of Latin include *aurea mediocritas* (the golden mean between extremes), the journey or quest, and the *summum bonum* (the greatest good).

Moreover, Latin can serve as a Rosetta stone for unlocking an understanding of our cultural heritage. It can help students understand that the Roman empire and its ideas dominated thought and action in both Western and Eastern parts of Europe and into Asia and Africa and that its traces are profound not only in continental Europe, but also in Britain, where Roman history is still definitive in all ways of life. The idea of cities and the infrastructure to maintain them, including the engineering marvel of the aqueduct, was a Roman contrivance. We understand our pagan history through the Greek and Roman myths and religion, as well as through ancient science and medicine. Our literature, art, and music today are heavily dependent on classical ideas, forms, and allusions to provide continuity and substance to our understanding of the world.

CONCLUSION

This opening chapter has provided an overview of the book, outlining its purpose, audience, and organization. It also has

focused on the use of the Integrated Curriculum Model as an organizing tool that promotes differentiation for the study of Latin by gifted learners proposed in the book. The model is described along with the application to the curriculum proposed. An alignment section demonstrates how the study of Latin fits with the new NAGC Gifted Programming Standards as well. Finally, the chapter offers a rationale for teaching Latin to gifted learners that defines the value of both the Latin language and the Roman culture.

REFERENCES AND RESOURCES

American Association for the Advancement of Science. (1990). *Science for all Americans: Project 2061*. New York, NY: Oxford University Press.

Coffin, D. (1981). *Classics: Essay on teaching able students*. (ERIC Clearance No. SP019263)

Draper, J. B., & Hicks, J. H. (2002). *Foreign language enrollments in public secondary schools, Fall 2000. Summary report*. Alexandria, VA: American Council on the Teaching of Foreign Languages.

Everitt, A. (2001). *Cicero*. New York, NY: Random House.

Harrington-Lueker, D. (1992). Latin redux. *Executive Educator, 14*(8), 21–25.

McManus, B. (2001). The Vroma project: Community and context for Latin teaching and learning. *CALICO Journal, 18*(2), 249–268.

Paul, R., & Elder, L. (2011). *Critical thinking: Tools for taking charge of your learning and your life*. Upper Saddle River, NJ: Prentice Hall.

Perkins, D. (1992). Selecting fertile themes for integrated learning. In H. H. Jacob (Ed.), *Interdisciplinary curriculum: Design and implementation* (pp. 67–75). Alexandria, VA: Association for Supervision and Curriculum Development.

Prager, R. (2000). Introductory language: Opening new doors. *Middle School Journal, 31*(4), 29–33.

Shelton, S. (2000). Breathing new life into a dead language: Teaching Latin online. *T.H.E. Journal, 27*(8), 64–66.

Sher, B. T. (1993). *A guide to key science concepts*. Williamsburg, VA: Center for Gifted Education.

Van Stekelenburg, A. (1984). *Classics for the gifted: Evaluation*. Paper presented at the International Conference: Education for the Gifted, Stellenbosch, Republic of South Africa.

VanTassel-Baska, J. 1986. Effective curriculum and instructional models for talented students. *Gifted Child Quarterly, 30*, 164–169.

VanTassel-Baska, J. 1987. A case for the teaching of Latin to the verbally talented. *Roeper Review, 9*, 159–61.

VanTassel-Baska, J. (Ed.). (1998). *Excellence in educating gifted and talented learners* (3rd ed.). Denver, CO: Love.

VanTassel-Baska, J. (2004). Quo Vadis? Laboring in the classical vineyards: An optimal challenge for gifted secondary students. *Journal of Secondary Gifted Education, 15*, 56–60.

VanTassel-Baska, J., & Little, C. (2011). *Content-based curriculum for the gifted*. Waco, TX: Prufrock Press.

VanTassel-Baska, J., & Olszewski-Kubilius, P. (Eds.). (1988). *Profiles of precocity*. New York, NY: Teachers College Press.

VanTassel-Baska, J., & Stambaugh, T. (2006). *Comprehensive curriculum for gifted learners* (3rd ed.). Needham Heights, MA: Allyn & Bacon.

Ward, V. (1981). *Differential education for the gifted*. Ventura County, CA: Office of the Superintendent of Schools.

Wheelock, F. M. (1995). *Wheelock's Latin*. New York, NY: HarperCollins.

Wheelock, F. M. (2000). *Wheelock's Latin* (6th ed.). New York, NY: HarperCollins.

Wilhelm, M. P., & Wilhelm, R. M. (1991). *Bringing the classics to life*. Humanities, *12*(1), 13–16.

CHAPTER 2

A LINGUIST'S PERSPECTIVE ON LATIN LANGUAGE AND CULTURE

BY AARON NITZKIN, PH.D.

> *Vivit duater qui etiam amat res vades.*
> He lives doubly who also enjoys the past.
>
> —Martial

INTRODUCTION

What does it mean to be human? Language and culture, which are hardly separable, are probably the most distinguishing traits of humanity. Language may be the most powerful and sophisticated tool yet "created by" (evolved in) human beings and the most sophisticated ability of the human nervous system. Many scholars suspect (but cannot prove) that language was responsible for transforming human minds into the all-purpose imaginative devices that they are today (Mithen, 2005). Language is a most essential aspect of human interpersonal communication—our primary tool for creating and managing our relationships with each other and with all of the institutions that make up a society. Moreover, language enables human beings to creatively shape and pass on knowledge, practices, and ways of thinking from one person or generation to the next in the form of memes that carry cultural ideas.

Language and culture are as fundamental to the human condition as cells and organs are to the genetic makeup of the body. We are all social beings belonging to a certain culture; we define ourselves with words and concepts such as *student, teacher, friend, artist, athlete, American, Black, White, smart, dumb*, etc. We talk to ourselves in our heads all day long, using the words of our culture, labeling people we see and things we experience with the ideas of our culture—"fun," "cool," "sketchy," "hot," "beast," whatever. These are all *concepts* that we could not apply to ourselves without language and culture. They are not simply labels for the way things are. People in different cultures may have different words, different concepts—and different identities. In traditional India, a teacher is a "guru," which is said to mean "spiritual friend"—and traditionally all education was considered spiritual. In Mandarin Chinese, a "master" of any skill can be called a *shi-fu*, "knowledge-father"—and students of traditional Chinese arts do indeed relate to their teachers as parents in many ways, even living in their *shi-fu*'s household. In these ways, language shapes our perceptions and relationships and enables us to fit into our culture(s).

By studying language and culture, we learn about how and why human beings and their societies are the way they are—especially about some of the uniquely human behaviors—things like praying, writing satirical science fiction, undergoing hypnotherapy, rapping, declaring war, and enjoying musical theatre. It is impossible to account for or understand any of these things in purely material terms; they depend primarily on the human ability to perceive, attribute, create, and manipulate *meaning*. Human beings live in a world constructed of meaning and populated with intangible entities made of meaning, such as love, God, differential equations, and pathos. These things are, in some sense, made not of protons, neutrons, and electrons, but of language and culture.

In fact, I would argue, perhaps against the spirit of our day, that the most important thing in the universe to most people is meaning. Yes, everyone needs food and shelter, but we live *for* meaning. We live *for* ideas and feelings, such as "salvation," "justice," "love," "honor," and "the good." The study of language and culture intersects a great deal with the sciences of learning, psychology, politics, and sociology, among others. Think about how you define and manage your own emotions, relationships, and social being: thank yous, apologies, insults, compliments, prayers, blessings, curses, and agreements are fundamentally made of language and culture. And so are laws, political platforms, and declarations of war.

The study of language and culture can provide great benefits for humanity. It has the potential to enable us to educate people better, take care of their mental health better, and generally manage social and political lives better.

The study of language and culture has always revolved around one center of gravity—the idea of cultural relativity—which is the idea that how one understands, perceives, feels, and thinks depends on what culture one lives in. This important realization has shaped all thought relating to the differences between cultures for the past 50 years and more. The sections that follow present some of the questions people have been asking and trying to answer.

To what degree does the cultural relativity of language shape culturally specific minds? Do people who speak different languages think differently? How much so? Do people who speak different languages experience the world differently? Is the shape of the mind determined by language or does it merely reflect it? How do linguistic differences affect cross-cultural communication? To what degree is translation possible? How much do we misunderstand each other and what can or should we do about it—especially in the context of classrooms, medical care, and courts of law? To what degree does the structure and vocabulary of a language embody a specific culture—beliefs, values, and ways of thinking and doing? How different, actually, are the ideas represented by words from one culture to another?

In Sweden, people have an attitude toward personal quality that is difficult to translate into English. Swedish people traditionally feel that a person should not try to appear better than other people, especially in terms of their appearance in public. It is regarded as socially inappropriate to stick out, even in a good way; you don't want to look like you think you're better than anyone. I was amused, during my time in Sweden, to see that the news anchors on Swedish TV wore old sweaters with threads sticking out, had on unprofessional or no makeup, and had bad hair. This value system is expressed in the Swedish saying *lagom ar bäst* (so-so is best).

The most famous and controversial theory about language and culture based on cultural relativity is the Sapir-Whorf hypothesis (Carroll, 1956). And although everybody should know about it, and ponder it deeply, I should say that it is most often misrepresented. Neither Edward Sapir nor his student Benjamin Lee Whorf presented the idea as a "hypothesis." They both studied the ways in which languages encode ways of thinking about the world and speculated about whether a language that carves up the world in a particular way might enforce a certain way of thinking on speakers of that language. Neither one of them was actually naïve enough to argue for the "hard" version of the so-called "Sapir-Whorf hypothesis"—that language absolutely determines the limits of thought. Strangely, many teachers and amateur philosophers do seem to debate whether this is true, but most linguists and anthropologists simply agree with the "soft" version of the hypothesis—that language influences thought in a powerful way but does not absolutely determine it. There is still plenty of room to argue about the details!

There are at least two ways in which you can think of this hypothesis in terms of the vocabulary of a language. One idea is that languages have words that cannot be translated because they represent culture-specific ideas; further examples include the American word "fun," the Sanskrit word "dharma," and the Greek "agapé." The other idea about vocabulary is that what people can perceive and think could be limited to the differences expressed by the vocabulary of their language. Different languages have words for different sets of colors, family members, spatial relationships, and many other things. For example, there is only one word in Swedish for both "squid" and "octopus"—*blekfisk*. I once had a difficult time convincing a Swedish friend that they are different animals!

People have done a lot of research on how this works for color words in various languages, beginning with the famous experiments of Berlin and Kay (Kay & McDaniel, 1978). It turns out that the set of color words that exists in a particular language does affect the way a speaker of that language classifies colored objects, but it is still possible for people to perceive color differences for which their language has no words.

Boaz, Sapir, and Whorf were all interested in the idea that a language's grammatical structure could embody ways of seeing the world. In the most famous example, Whorf pointed out that the Native American Hopi language does not have present, past, and future verb tenses (Whorf, 1950). Instead, Hopi marks verbs for the real (the here and now) versus the unreal (past, future, and imagination). Moreover, Whorf claimed that Hopi nouns described "things" as processes rather than static objects. Does this mean that the Hopi experience time and reality differently than we do? Whorf speculated that a Hopi child would be able to understand Einstein's theory of relativity more easily than an English speaker. Most linguists today are skeptical about claims like this. For one thing, we now understand that languages that don't express time through verb tenses do it in other ways, such as by beginning sentences with words like "yesterday." Secondly, Whorf's best example of a noun-process word in Hopi was a word for a "spring" (as in water) whose structure seems similar (to me) to the English word "waterfall." Things often look more exotic than they really are when you are researching alien languages.

Do people live in linguistically shaped "reality tunnels"? What misunderstandings between cultures do we fail to recognize if we don't take cultural relativity into consideration? How do these differences impact people's abilities to participate equally in the institutions of a society? There is plenty of evidence that misunderstandings based on language and culture can interfere with people's educations and rights in a society.

MORPHOLOGY AND CULTURE: GRAMMATICAL CONCEPTS

There are two different things called "morphology." Morphology concerns (1) the formation of words through historical, social, and cultural processes; and (2) the changes in the forms of words that are part of the grammar of a language—such as changing the endings of nouns and verbs to express grammatical information such as number, gender, tense, aspect, and case. I have already discussed some examples of the second kind of morphology, in connection with the Sapir-Whorf Hypothesis and the Hopi. Let us look at one very different example. There are many intriguing examples of grammatical morphology that seem to express culture. Bantu languages provide some great examples because they possess what linguists call "noun classes." Noun classes are basically what we call "gender" in Indo-European languages (that a noun may have a masculine or feminine grammatical identity, such as in French, Spanish, Italian, and Russian)—except that there are more than 2–3 noun classes, and they are more meaningful and diverse than grammatical gender.

MORPHOLOGY, SEMANTICS, AND CULTURE: ETYMOLOGICAL METAPHOR

Why do we say "understand"? I mean, what does standing under things have to do with understanding them? Is it because if you stand under something you can see otherwise hidden parts of it? I don't know, but I am extremely curious, especially because there is also a Sanskrit word for "understand," *avagacchati*, which literally means "go under." I strongly suspect that this is a case of my favorite aspect of historical linguistics—what I call **etymological metaphor**. Etymology is the study of word origins. Etymological metaphors are metaphors in the origins of words. Take the word "discover"; it means to take the cover off of something. It relies on several metaphors, such as *knowledge is vision* and *meaning is substance*. These metaphors exist independently of the individual words, they are productive; so in English, you can "twist" meaning, "condense" it, "fill" things with it, and empty things of it. Most, perhaps all, of these metaphors exist in other languages, but they express themselves uniquely in each.

You can find etymological metaphors most easily by looking at fancy words for abstract things. In English, many fancy words for abstracts come from Latin and contain metaphors: *comprehend* (understand) literally means "to grasp together"; *aversion* (dislike) literally means "turning-away from"; *perspicacity* (insight) literally means "looking through" something. Of course, *insight* literally means "seeing into" and that one is from Anglo-Saxon. Anglo-Saxon words, such as *overlook* and *foresee*, are often more transparent than Latinate words. The sharp reader may have noticed that many of these words are based on metaphors of vision. The metaphors for mental activity based on vision are among the most common, universal, and translatable of all etymological metaphors, and a perfect example of **conceptual metaphor**.

Etymological metaphors are just one kind of conceptual metaphor, or metaphorical idea that gets expressed in many words and phrases in a language. For example, consider some of the English words and phrases based on the conceptual metaphor "mental activity is vision": *foresight, prescience, metacognitive.*

Metaphor reveals that all language is poetry, because it is an area of linguistics that shows how deeply history and culture can be wrapped up in a language.

LANGUAGE, CULTURE, AND HISTORY—ENGLISH AND LATIN

In the previous section, we saw that the words of a language can tell us a lot about the culture that created them. But what about when the words of a language come from a different culture? For example, the English words *brainwash, assassin,* and *slogan* come from Chinese, Arabic, and Gaelic, respectively; so do they tell us about the culture of English speakers, or the culture of the language they originally came from? The answer is that such words may not only express both the culture that donated the word, and the culture that borrowed it, but more interestingly, such words tell us about the history of the interactions between those cultures; they may tell us stories of wars, religious missions, great explorers, and more.

English has borrowed many words from many languages—perhaps more than any other language in the world—but there is only one language that has given so many words to English that many, perhaps most, Americans mistakenly believe that it is the root language from which English was born—and that is Latin, of course. It is estimated that 60% of English vocabulary can be traced to Latin, even though English is not a direct descendant of Latin as French, Spanish, and Italian are. Before I tell the epic story of cultural exchange that accounts for this odd situation, I should add that this statistic is slightly deceptive; although 60% of English vocabulary may be Latinate, the core vocabulary of English is still by and large Germanic. What I mean is that most of the basic down-to-Earth words, such as pronouns, prepositions, and one-syllable words for simple everyday objects and actions do not come from Latin, but rather from Anglo-Saxon and Norse. If you avoid talking about anything scientific, religious, political, legal, academic, high-class, or philosophical, you can conceivably speak without using any words from Latin. That is the first and most general indication of the cultural-historical relationship between English and Latin—English speakers had relatively little in the way of science, politics, law, education, or literacy before encountering Latin. Religion and philosophy are another story—the Anglo-Saxons had their own at one time, but it was, for the most part, replaced by Roman Christianity.

The relationship between English and Latin begins long before the Germanic tribes interacted with Latin speakers, or even before either group existed. Their relationship begins, according to historical linguists, more than 6,000 years ago, roughly somewhere between Eastern Turkey (previously called Anatolia) and Chechnya—between the Black and Caspian seas. Linguists are fairly certain that English and Latin, as well as many other languages of Europe and South Asia, are all descended from a common ancestral language that linguists call Proto-Indo-European (PIE). Surprisingly, although there are no records of PIE, and we can't even know for sure that it existed, we nevertheless believe that we know quite a bit about the culture that spoke it, and some of the specifics nicely reveal a common heritage shared by the Anglo-Saxons and the Romans.

By comparing the vocabularies of many Indo-European languages (such as Sanskrit, Greek, Gaelic, Farsi, Russian, Latin, and English), linguists have discovered which words in these languages appear to be related to each other, such as *pater* (Latin), *father* (English), and *pitar* (Sanskrit). Then, we conclude that these words are all mutated forms of one original word in Proto-Indo-European. The words in the descendent languages are called cognates (literally "born-together" from Latin). By comparing many words in this way, linguists can figure out what things the original Indo-Europeans had words for (such as fathers). Interestingly, these things include:

- a father/sky god;
- ritual sacrifice;
- cows, horses, and dogs;
- wheeled carts, but not chariots;
- agriculture; and
- oral heroic poetry.

We can conclude that these things are part of the shared cultural heritage of all of the many Indo-European peoples, from Ireland to Afghanistan. And that is where the cultural-linguistic relationship between the Romans and English begins.

Unfortunately, we don't know much more than that about Indo-European culture or language before the development of civilizations and written records. We don't know a lot about what happened between Proto-Indo-European and the documented historical records of Latin, Greek, and English, which first appear thousands of years later.

The first period in which Latin words became part of English was before English was English—before the Germanic tribes of Angles, Saxons, and Jutes invaded England in 450 CE. Linguists have figured out that there are a few hundred Latin words in English that were probably "borrowed" by these tribes before they invaded England. How can we tell that? There are many kinds of circumstantial evidence, such as whether the words also exist in other Germanic languages that were spoken on the continent at that time, and whether the words have gone through certain sound-changes that occurred in the Germanic languages or Latin at roughly known times. But historical linguistics is certainly not an exact science. In any case, here are some of the words that were probably borrowed into English from Latin by the Germanic tribes before they invaded England, given below in their Old English and modern forms. They are quite different in kind from the words that would be borrowed from Latin a few hundred years later.

Words associated with		
Military Campaigns:	**Trade, Especially Foods:**	**Roman Architectural Technology:**
weall (wall), *pytt* (pit), *straet* (street), *mil* (mile)	*win* (wine), *ciese* (cheese), *pipor* (pepper)	*cealc* (chalk), *pic* (pitch), *tigele* (tile)

Unlike future borrowings, these are not abstract, intellectual, multi-syllabic words; they are concrete things, words that a Germanic trader, soldier, or builder might bring home from his encounters with Romans— but also words representing innovations of Roman civilization, or at least things previously unknown, or different, among the Germanic peoples.

The second time that the English borrowed words from Latin was during the Christianization of England. Over a century after the Angles, Saxons, and Jutes invaded England, Pope Gregory sent a mission to England, in 597 CE. Although this was not the first time the Anglo-Saxons had come into contact with Christianity, it marked the beginning of the Christianization of England, when the Anglo-Saxon king Aethelbert of Kent converted to Christianity in 601 CE. Following his conversion came many more priests and monks to England, and they brought many Latin words, several hundred of which became part of English over the next 100 years or so, including these:

- **Christianity:** *abbot, alms, altar, angel, ark, cleric, mass,* etc.
- **Words for clothing, food, and literature introduced by Roman Christians:** *cap, sock, beet, lentil, radish, verse, meter, gloss,* etc.

The cultural weight of these words seems obvious, although there is more than one message to be read out of them. On the one hand, there are words that only apply to Christianity, such as *cleric* and *mass*; on the other hand there are words that don't technically have anything to do with Christianity, but came to us because Christianity represented Roman civilization, which possessed more technology, education, and international trade than the Anglo-Saxons of early England. We can see similar cultural-linguistic phenomena today when we look at the words borrowed from European colonial languages (such as Spanish and French) into local languages all over the world, such as the Spanish words *piscin* (swimming pool) and *dios* (god) that appear in Yucatec Maya, and English words such as *taksi* (taxi) and *ripot* (report) in Swahili.

Other Latin words made it into Old English in less direct ways that also highlight the importance of culture and history in language evolution. For example, the words "cross" (crucifix) and "candle," which originally came from Latin, were probably borrowed by the Anglo-Saxons from the Irish Celtic language because Ireland had received Roman Christian missionaries and their Latin centuries before the Anglo-Saxons did. Although the Anglo-Saxons remained largely pagan until after St. Augustine's mission to England in 597 CE, they were exposed to Christianity and Latin through their contacts with the Irish before then, and throughout the Anglo-Saxon period.

During the last 200 years of the first millennium CE, English was shaped not so much by Latin as by the Norse invasion and settlement of half of England. In fact, linguists still debate whether English should be considered a *creole* language, the result of the mixing of two parent languages. Could English perhaps be the creole offspring of Anglo-Saxon and Norse, or—due to the next stage in its history—of Anglo-Saxon and French? This brings us to the most often remembered event in the history of English or England—the invasion of England by the Norman French under the leadership of William "the Conqueror."

Before recounting the linguistic consequences of the Norman conquest of England, it is worth remarking briefly on the origins of Norman French. Most people know that French is a descendant of Latin; it is Latin itself, changed over the past 2,000 years by various forces including Germanic and Celtic languages, which used to be or still are spoken within its territory or on its borders. France is named after the Germanic Franks and Normandy after the Norse-men who invaded and settled there only a couple of centuries before the French-speaking Normans invaded England. However, the territory we call France had first been settled by the Romans more than 1000 years before the Normans invaded England, so French was always primarily a Roman(ce) language—albeit one that borrowed from both Germanic and Celtic languages, which is why it sounds so different from Italian and Spanish.

After the Normans conquered England under William, all English aristocracy, clergy, government officers, and lawyers spoke French for approximately 300 years. Not one King of England was even fluent in English for more than 200 years; King Edward I (1272–1307) was the first to speak English at all, and the English Parliament didn't officially take up English again until 1360. Latin was the official language of English Christianity and most official documents were written by priest-scribes in either Latin or Norman French.

Most of the population of England continued to speak primarily English throughout this period. Nevertheless, many English people (e.g., tradesmen, clerks, priests, etc.) learned French in order to carry out their business. And English must have been a necessary language for a large proportion of knights, clergy, and tax officers. It is reasonable to presume that the vast amount of Latinate French and Latin vocabulary that entered English during this time period did so largely due to the needs of everyday English people and lesser aristocracy to communicate with each other about matters of law, business, governance, and religion. As one might expect, the French-derived vocabulary of English is still dominated by words belonging to these areas of activity—and also by words associated with the lifestyles of the aristocracy. These words can be seen in the table below.

Governmental	Military	Judicial System	Ecclesiastical	Cuisine
count, heraldry, fine, noble, parliament	*battle, ally, alliance, ensign, admiral, navy, aid, gallant, march, enemy, escape, peace*	*judge, jury, plaintiff, justice, court, suit, defendant, crime, felony, murder petty/ petit, attorney, marriage* (Anglo-Saxon *wedding*), *heir*	*miracle, preach, pray, sermon, virgin, saint, friar/frere*	*sauce, boil, filet, soup, pastry, fry, roast, toast*

Because French is a direct descendant of Latin, the French-ifying of English can be considered a third wave of Latin entering English. It is also the largest, accounting for at least half of modern English vocabulary.

The domination of England by French faded away fairly quickly from the late 13th through the 14th century, but this was not the last wave of Latin to enter English. The final stage of English Latinization—and perhaps the one that is most purely cultural in origins—began during the 17th century and continues to this day. Up until the 17th century, English was, in most people's eyes, a barbarian, or at least a low-class, language. Although the Anglo-Saxons had created great works of poetry and history, such as *Beowulf* and the *Anglo-Saxon Chronicle*, it was not a language of philosophy, politics, religion, law, science, or scholarship in general. The first Bible in English, John Wycliff's, was written in the 14th century and was considered heretical, but the English Bible didn't become common until after the printing of the King James Bible in 1610. So when English began to be used more and more for all kinds of literature, around this time, writers had to invent new English words, or borrow them from French, Latin, Greek, and sometimes other languages, such as Arabic, Persian, and Gaelic. Some of these are in the table below.

Latin	*Greek*	*Arabic via Spanish*
agile, abdomen, anatomy, area, capsule, compensate, dexterity, discus, disc/disk, excavate, expensive, fictitious, gradual, habitual, insane, janitor, meditate, notorious, orbit, peninsula, physician, superintendent, ultimate, vindicate	(many of these via Latin) anonymous, atmosphere, autograph, catastrophe, climax, comedy, critic, data, ecstasy, history, ostracize, parasite, pneumonia, skeleton, tonic, tragedy	alcove, algebra, zenith, algorithm, almanac, azimuth, alchemy, admiral

Scholars and specialists in all sciences continue to create English words out of Latin and Greek elements to this day. They use the Latin and Greek roots because of their cultural associations—because they represented knowledge, wisdom, and culture. The reasons that these languages have had that cultural significance for English speakers especially included the military successes of the Roman Empire and the Normans, the success of Christianity, and the very limited assortment of foreign literature available to Western Europeans during the Dark Ages—making Latin the only gateway to knowledge for most people in that place and time. The fabric of the English language is a tapestry of cultural history woven from many different threads.

CONCLUSION

Latin is the largest single source of the language of 2,000 years of Western European and American civilization and scholarship; it is part of the foundation of the Western mind. It is an inheritor and transmitter of knowledge and ideas from many ancient cultures. At the same time, the study of language and culture also reveals that the sources of our cultures are many and varied and the history of their development one of constant change and exchange. We all continue to reshape our languages, cultures, and identities on a daily basis, through the metaphors we use, the words we coin, and through our poetry, stories, and songs. To create with language is to participate in the reshaping of your world.

DISCUSSION QUESTIONS

1. Do you agree that language and culture are what makes human beings different from other animals? Why or why not?
2. Research animal communication systems and culture and discuss why or why not animals have the same capability to do things with meaning that human beings have.
3. Do you agree or disagree that meaning is the most important thing to human beings. Why or why not? Use examples from history and your experience to back up your answer.
4. In what ways could we use language and culture to make the world a better place?
5. Do people who speak different languages think, experience, or perceive the world differently? What evidence suggests that this is true or false?
6. Discuss how linguistic or cultural differences might affect people's ability to get a good education, fair legal treatment, medical care, or a job.

7. How does English, or another language, encode the values of some culture? Try brainstorming all of the words we use to describe people in English (or another language) and use that list to figure out what we think is important about people in our culture.
8. How does language affect thinking? Does it control it, limit it, or merely provide the means to express it? Defend your point of view.

ACTIVITIES

1. Look up the origins of the word *prescience*, using at least two different online sources: Online Etymological Dictionary (http://www.etymonline.com) and Wiktionary (http://www.wiktionary.com). Discuss the results. What do they tell you about history and culture? What do they tell you about the reliability of online sources?
2. Review the list of the vocabulary of Proto-Indo-European found at the University of Texas at Austin website (http://www.utexas.edu/cola/centers/lrc/ielex/PokornyMaster-X.html). Consider that every word on that list must have survived from 6,000 years ago up to the present day in many Indo-European languages. What sorts of words appear on the list? Why would those words last while others changed? Can you tell anything more about Indo-European culture by examining this list of words?

REFERENCES AND RESOURCES

Baugh, A. C., & Cable, T. (2002). *A history of the English language* (5th ed.). London, England: Routledge.

Carroll, J. B. (Ed.). (1956). *Language, thought, and reality: Selected writing of Benjamin Lee Whorf.* Cambridge, MA: The MIT Press.

Kay, P., & McDaniel, K. (1978). The linguistic significance of the meanings of basic color terms. *Language, 54*(3), 610–646.

Mithen, S. J. (2005). *The singing Neanderthals: The origins of music, language, mind and body.* Cambridge, MA: Harvard University Press.

Whorf, B. L. (1950). An American Indian model of the universe. *International Journal of American Linguistics, 16,* 67–72.

CHAPTER 3

THE ROLE OF THE LATIN LANGUAGE IN THE WORLD

> *Vox audita perit, littera scripta manet.*
> The heard word is lost, the written letter abides.
>
> —Anonymous

INTRODUCTION

Latin is one of more than 7,000 languages that exist in the world today. More than any other language, it has influenced the development of language and culture in all Western civilizations. Only Sanskrit, Hebrew, and ancient Greek hold a comparable status in influencing current day languages. Although Latin shares many features of the Greek language (i.e., grammar and vocabulary), it maintains a distinctive alphabet and language structure shared by many other languages today, including English.

RELATIONSHIP OF LATIN TO ENGLISH

It is important to acknowledge that, even though English is derived from West Germanic on the Indo-European language tree, it shares many commonalities with Latin, the progenitor (*pro* means "for" and *genitor* means "father"; progenitor = forefather) of the Romance languages. These include Spanish, French, Portuguese, Romanian, and Italian, among other European languages.

First of all, *complex English vocabulary is based on Latin in form and meaning.* Almost all words of three syllables and more (90%) in English have a Greek and/or Latin root. Many also have a prefix or suffix that is derived from Latin and therefore, the reader who knows those stems can discern meaning more easily. Most so-called SAT words have a Latin origin. Consequently, vocabulary tests in English favor those who have studied Latin or who at least know the roots and stems of the language.

A few examples of this phenomenon follow.

- Collaboration (5 syllables)—prefix is *co* (n) meaning "together" in Latin, the root is *laboro* (v.), meaning "to work"—the word means "a working together" in English. *Tion* is a noun ending. Example sentence: The **collaboration** between the jazz musicians as they adjusted to each other's improvisations was magnificent.

- Communication (5 syllables)—prefix is derived from *cum* (prep.) in Latin meaning "with," root is from *nuncio* (v.) meaning "to announce"—the word means "the act of speaking with each other." Example sentence: The family worked to improve **communication** about who needed to be where and when.

- Derisive (3 syllables)—prefix is *de* (prep.) meaning "from" or "about," and the root is *riso* meaning to laugh—the word means "scornful or making fun of" (laughing at). *Ive* is an adjective ending. Example sentence: The critic was **derisive** about the performance of the dancers and poked fun at the choreographer's decisions.

- Adventure (3 syllables)—prefix is *ad* (prep.) meaning "to" or "toward," and the root is *venio* meaning to come—the word literally means "to come forward, or a step out to take on something exceptional." Example sentence: The young graduate could not wait to take on his study abroad **adventure**.

- Beneficent (4 syllables)—prefix is *bene* (adv.) meaning well and the root is *facio* (v.) meaning "to make or do"—the word describes someone who "does good things for others." *Ent* is an adjectival ending. Example sentence: My aunt was very **beneficent** toward me, granting gifts and the benefit of her wisdom.

Studying words in respect to their component Latin roots and stems provides important insights into English vocabulary that can enhance writing and oral communication.

Secondly, *English grammar is based on the structure of Latin syntax.* We understand that structure better by seeing it applied to Latin with the inflected endings that reveal the form and function of particular words in sentences. These forms reveal more information about a noun than can be found in English sentences, such as use and purpose. In the case of verbs, these inflected endings reveal the tense and voice. An example may illustrate this principle.

> *Puella ab alienis et ad suam matrem currit.*
> **Translation:** The girl runs away from strangers and toward her mother.
> **Grammatical analysis:** The ending of the short *a* in *puella* indicates it is the subject of the sentence. The present tense of the verb is used to indicate time in the here and now. The preposition *ab* which means away from always takes the ablative case following it, as does the noun here meaning strangers. The conjunction "and" appears as a conjunction (from *cum* meaning "with" and *jungo* "to join") to emphasize the opposite direction in the sentence—*ad suam matrem (toward her mother)*. The preposition *ad* always takes the accusative case following it.

The special endings of the nouns convey their gender, number, and case; the form of the verb indicates tense, voice, person, and number. These grammatical forms clarify how words are employed in Latin to make meaning. Figure 2 explains the terms and how they apply to the language to create meaning.

As in Latin, English has eight parts of speech, multiple functions for nouns in sentences, and a set of two voices and six tenses for verbs. Sentence order is different in that Latin often places the verb form at the end of the sentence rather than after the subject, where it is stated in an English sentence. However, the inflected (literally *bent inward* or changing) endings of nouns provide clues to their order in the sentence and connection to other words such as prepositions.

Nouns

Gender—in Latin there are three genders into which all nouns are classified: feminine, masculine, and neuter. Adjectives agree with a noun and take the same gender.

Number—in Latin there are singular and plural noun forms, referring to whether one item/person or multiple items/people are referred to. Adjectives again, must agree with the noun they reference, indicating the number of people performing an action.

Case—in Latin, case determines the function of a noun in a sentence, whether it is a subject or an object and what kind. There are five main Latin cases. The nominative (from the Latin word "nomen" meaning name) is used for subjects and predicate nominatives (e.g., The boy is happy, both boy and happy are in the nominative because the boy is the subject and happy is an adjective that describes him). The accusative (from the Latin word "ad" meaning toward and "causativus" meaning something caused) is reserved for direct objects, and objects of some prepositions (e.g., *ad*, toward). For example, in the sentence, "The girl kicks the ball toward the house," the ball would be the direct object because it receives the action of the verb. Likewise the house would also be accusative, because the word for toward (ad) takes the accusative after it. (See the sample Latin sentence on p. 37.)

The next important case to discuss is the genitive (from the Latin genus, generis for type or kind) which is used for possessives. This kind of noun is used in place of the word "of" or the apostrophe s in English. For example, in the sentence "the girl's dog ran away," "girl's" would be in the genitive, because it shows to whom the dog belonged. The dative case (from the Latin do, dare—to give) is used for the indirect object with verbs of giving, telling, or showing. For example, in the sentence, "I gave the queen's daughter a rose," the subject would be "I" (nominative), the direct object would be "rose" (accusative), the possessive would be "queen's" (genitive) and the indirect object would be "daughter" (dative), because she received the direct object. Likewise, if you said, "I showed the book to him," the book would be the direct object, but "him" would be the indirect object. The last of the most important five cases to discuss is the ablative, which is used (among other things) for the object of those prepositions which don't take the accusative (e.g., cum [with]). Therefore, in the sentence, "I walked with my friend," "my friend" would be in the ablative case.

Verbs

Person—the forms of pronouns and whether they are referring to oneself ("I, we" are the first person forms, singular and plural) or to you/you all (second person), or to others (he, she, or it/they are in the third person).

FIGURE 2. Basic grammatical structures in Latin

> **Number**—whether the pronoun is singular or plural (e.g., I vs. we, you vs. you all, she vs. they).
>
> **Tense**—the time when the verb or action takes place in a sentence or text. The basic tenses in Latin are present ("The girl walks the dog."), imperfect ("The girl was walking the dog."), perfect ("The girl walked the dog."), and future (the girl will walk the dog).
>
> **Voice**—whether the action is active or passive, with the subject doing something or having something done to it. An active example would be "The girl carried the water." The same sentence expressed in a passive sentence would be "The water was carried by the girl." Note that in a passive sentence, the subject does not actually do the verb, it is completely passive while other parts of the sentence act upon it.
>
> **FIGURE 2.** *continued*

Thirdly, *many English meters are derived from Latin poetic forms like iambic pentameter or dactylic hexameter.* Meter refers to the rhythm of the words and the rules that command their pronunciation and accents. Great English poets such as Shakespeare, Milton, and Pope owe much to the Roman poets who mastered the art of meter and employed it rigorously to all their work. For example, Vergil wrote his epic *Aeneid* in nearly 10,000 lines of dactylic hexameter, a particularly popular meter that required six feet of 2–3 syllables each, with a specific metrical pattern.

Finally, *English usage principles are related to Latin syntactical structures.* For example, the rule of subject-verb agreement (e.g., "she runs" versus "they run") is similar to the application of that principle in Latin where endings agree in number from subject to verb. Our case endings for pronouns are cognates to Latin's inflected endings. Thus, the indefinite pronoun *who* may be used in the nominative form when it serves as subject or predicate nominative but must change to *whom* when it becomes the direct or indirect object of a verb, mirroring the "-m" accusative ending in Latin.

Sentence types—declarative, interrogative, and imperative—all come to us from Latin, in which the mixing of these forms was routine in both speech and writing. The construction of the complexity of sentences also is derived from Latin, in which the careful use of clauses dictated more complex patterns of communication.

Therefore, because we have inherited both words and language structures from the Romans, our deep, intellectual knowledge of English is inextricably (*in* = not, *extrico* = pull out; meaning "not able to be pulled out") linked to understanding Latin and how it works as a language.

THE INDO-EUROPEAN LANGUAGE TREE

Latin is the main language from which all Romance languages are derived, including French, Spanish, Catalan, Portuguese, Romanian, and Italian. Latin is no longer spoken anywhere except The Vatican in Rome and in the Catholic Church, where it is still the official language. The language dominated all parts of the Roman Empire during the first four centuries across both Western and Eastern Europe. The languages cited evolved from Latin into their current forms today based on geography and cultural ties. Some of them, French in particular, have recently been discovered to have such lexical similarities that they could actually be considered a dialect of Latin (*Ethnologue*).

SPECIAL PHRASES AND ADAGES

The Romans were very fond of developing and using certain sayings over and over again as they explained the philosophy of being in the ancient world. Examples of some of these adages follow and are still used in conversation and writing today:

- *Mens sana in corpore sana.*
- *Suaviter in modo, fortiter in re.*
- *Ars longa, vita brevis.*
- *Fortes fortuna adiuvat.* (Vergil)
- *Falsus in unu, falsus in omnibus.*
- *Si vis pacem, para bellum.*
- *Pax vobiscum.*
- *Felicitas multos habet amicos.*
- *Caveat emptor.*
- *Sic transit Gloria mundi.*

You will have a chance to research these phrases during the units and uncover their application to today's world.

SENTENTIAE ANTIQUAE (ANCIENT OPINIONS)

Many Roman writers provided important ideas for our understanding of their thoughts and their world. These commentaries are preserved in longer literary pieces yet can be appreciated for their brevity and depth here.

A few of the most important writers and their thoughts follow:

- *Ex meis erroribus hominibus rectum iter demonstrare possum.* (Seneca)
- *Amor laudis homines trahit.* (Cicero)
- *Ratio me ducet, non fortuna.* (Livy)
- *Nihil sine magno labore vita mortalibus dat.* (Horace)
- *Si me duces, Musa (a personified inspiration), coronam magna cum laude capiam.* (Lucretius)
- *Verus amicus est alter idem.* (Cicero)
- *Nec tecum possum vivere nec sine te.* (Martial)
- *Inter bellum et pacem dubitabant.* (Tacitus)
- *Difficile est saturam non scribere.* (Juvenal)
- *Omnia mutantur; omnia fluunt; quod fuimus aut sumus, cras non erimus.* (Ovid)

These thoughts and feelings of ancient Roman writers are universal statements about life. Can you figure out what they mean in English and why the idea has survived?

ETYMOLOGY

Many Latin words come to us directly while others share a root or stem with ancient Greek as well. Knowing the source of words allows us to understand how they are used in modern English. Table 4 includes some common English words whose etymology lies in Latin.

As mentioned earlier in the vocabulary section, Latin roots and stems comprise many English words in many forms. Knowing these forms allows us to develop a more robust vocabulary in English.

TABLE 4
Latin Words and English Derivatives

Common Latin Verbs	English Words That Derive From Them
video (see)	provide
maneo (stay)	permanent
venio (come)	intervene
facio (make)	facile, fact
ago (do, drive)	agent, act
doceo (teach)	docile, doctor

GENRES

Roman writers created both great poetry and prose in the Latin language. Its greatest prose writers included Cicero, the orator; Livy, the historian; and Caesar, the general. Their words have been preserved for us to read and reflect on today.

Perhaps it is the Roman poets, however, whose contributions represent the greatest linguistic achievement. Vergil's epic poem *The Aeneid* and Horace's odes are two examples of important poetry, both within different genres.

Mythological beliefs in Rome extended to the beliefs of writers that the muses visited them as they tried to work and looked over their shoulders during the task, helping them with appropriate words and thoughts. These muses were nine in number and were responsible for different genres within poetry and beyond to different prose forms as well. Roman poets often formally invoked them in the context of a poem.

- **Calliope**, muse of epic poetry
- **Clio**, muse of history
- **Erato**, muse of love poetry
- **Euterpe**, muse of lyric poetry
- **Melpomene**, the muse of tragedy
- **Polyhymnia**, the muse of songs of praise to the gods
- **Terpsichore**, the muse of choral songs and dance
- **Thalia**, the muse of comedy
- **Urania**, the muse of astronomy

Roman writers also employed selected themes and tone that could be analyzed in their work. Praise of one's patron as well as the Roman state was a device used by most writers in Rome in order to ensure that their patronage continued. Fatalistic views of the world were often expressed, noting that men's fortunes were externally controlled by the gods. Aeneas, Vergil's hero, succeeds because he is protected by his mother Venus even though other gods such as Juno try to impede his progress.

Comedy and even satire were commonly employed in Roman work, inspired by the muse of comedy, Thalia. The playwrights Plautus and Terence used comedic devices in full measure. Juvenal employed satire to make fun of foolish people and aspects of Roman life that he considered flawed.

CONCLUSION

The language of Rome has a rich history and set of relationships with various places around the world. It influenced English grammar and usage rules and conventions. It also is the basis for much of our vocabulary as well as that of other Romance languages. Yet it is not spoken regularly anywhere in the world except the Vatican. However, there is a Finnish radio broadcast in Latin and several colloquia that are held around the world in Latin.

Many important ideas about how the world works have been inherited from the Latin language and incorporated into our conventional wisdom through adages and sayings, some that we can trace to famous Roman writers. It is a language worth studying to understand the linguistic heritage of Western civilization.

REFERENCES AND RESOURCES

Baade, E. C., Burgess, T. K., & Jenney, C. J. (1990). *Jenney's first year Latin.* Englewood Cliffs, NJ: Prentice Hall.

Hines, L. (1981). *Our Latin heritage: Book one.* Orlando, FL: Harcourt Brace Jovanovich.

Robbins, E. S., & Ashworth, K. R. (1995). *Discovering languages: Latin.* New York, NY: Amsco School Publications.

Rodgers, N. (2008). *Ancient Rome.* Leicester, England: Hermes House.

Wheelock, F. M. (2000). *Wheelock's Latin* (6th ed.). New York, NY: HarperCollins.

CHAPTER 4

HISTORY OF THE ROMAN EMPIRE
A STORY OF DEEDS AND MEN

> *Arma virumque cano.*
> I sing of arms and the man. . .
> —Vergil, Book I, *The Aeneid*

INTRODUCTION

The study of all things Roman must include an emphasis on the history of the development, reign, and decline of one of the greatest civilizations the world has ever known. Although we strive to emulate other aspects of the Roman civilization in art, literature, and even religious thought, the evolution of Rome as a mighty power in the Western world deserves commentary.

As most civilizations are marked by conflicts, so too was the Roman civilization. We can trace its development in three distinct periods from its mythological founding by the twins Romulus and Remus, who were supposedly raised by a she-wolf. The first period of rule, monarchy, began after the legendary leader, Romulus, murdered his brother Remus to become the first king of Rome. Rome had a grand total of seven kings on record, who ruled Rome from 753 BCE to 510 BCE. The second period of Rome, the Republic, saw the rise of wealthy, landed groups of men in government (the patricians) and the establishment of institutions like the Roman senate that provided order in the society even as it also was the period when Rome staged its most enduring conquests. The Empire is the third important period of Roman history, proceeding from the rise of Augustus as emperor in 27 BCE to the dissolution of the empire in 476 CE as the last emperor, ironically named Romulus Augustulus, abdicated. Many of the Roman ways of life continued without much change, however, for another 1,000 years, albeit in Byzantine form, throughout medieval Europe and beyond.

THE PERIOD OF MONARCHY

The founding of the city was carefully tied into mythology, justifying the divine will for Rome to flourish. The first myth is that of Aeneas, son of the goddess Venus, who brings the *penates*, household gods of Troy, to the area of Latium and founds the settlement near the city of Rome. Aeneas's son Ascanius founds Alba Longa, the area from which Romulus and Remus, Rome's mythological founders, would come.

Later in Roman mythology, the twins Romulus and Remus, children of the god Mars, grow up to build the city of Rome. This part of the story is woven into historical timelines, making the link between mythology and history inextricable in the discussion of Rome.

The Roman historian Livy (late first century BCE) wrote his history giving dates in AUC (*ab urbe condita* = from the founding of the city). His history starts with the Romulus founding of Rome. Plutarch, an early 2nd century CE Greek historian, wrote a biography of Romulus in which he dates the founding of Rome by referring to eclipses observed in Greece. For the Romans, the supernatural details did not detract from the history of the events. Equally supernatural stories and prodigies of nature abounded in accounts of other figures in Roman history, down to the emperors. The timeline below chronicles how Aeneas' story is incorporated as prehistory to the exploits of Romulus and Remus.

Timeline of Events Before the Founding of Rome
c. 1184 BCE   Fall of Troy
c. 1176 BCE   Aeneas founds Lavinium

c. 1152 BCE   Ascanius founds Alba Longa
c. 1152–753 BCE Kings of Alba Longa

Seven kings of Rome

- **Romulus** (c. 753–715 BCE) was the legendary founder of Rome with his brother Remus. They were left to die in the Tiber River after their mother Rhea Silvia, a Vestal Virgin who had mated with Mars (the Roman god of war), delivered them. They both were raised by a she-wolf who found and suckled them in the Lupercale, a cave near what was Alba Longa. They restored Numitor, the rightful ruler, to the throne in that region. Romulus and Remus decided to found a new city. Romulus wanted to found the city on the Palatine hill and saw 12 birds in the sky, considered an auspicious omen. Remus wanted to found the city on the Aventine hill, and saw six birds. The two brothers fought over what the omens meant and where the city should be founded, and in the fight, Romulus killed his brother and founded the city of Rome nearby. He served as the first king for 20 years.
- **Numa Pompilius** (c. 715–673) established many religious customs and rituals and reformed the Roman calendar. According to tradition, he received advice on how to rule from a nymph, or demigoddess, named Egeria, whom he later married. Again, mythology and history intertwine in the story of the Roman kings.
- **Tullus Hostilius** (c. 673–642 BCE) doubled the population of Rome, adding Alban nobles to the Senate, and built the Curia Hostilia, one of the ancient Senate houses. He was a warrior, but died after being struck by lightning because he performed a sacrifice to Jupiter incorrectly.
- **Ancus Marcius** (c. 642–617 BCE) was a grandson of Numa Pompilius and made his first order of business a campaign concerning the proper performance of religious rituals, using the guides his grandfather had created. Today, he is primarily remembered as a bridge builder. The bridge across the Tiber, the Pons Sublicius, is credited to him.
- **Tarquinius Priscus** or Tarquin the Elder (c. 616–579 BCE) was the first Etruscan king of Rome. Tarquinius Priscus had a Corinthian father, but more importantly, an influential wife named Tanaquil who orchestrated the rise of her husband to power, as well as the rise of Servius Tullius, the next king. Tarquin created 100 new

senators and expanded Rome. He also established the Roman games.

- **Servius Tullius** (c. 578–535 BCE) was the son-in-law of Tarquinius Priscus. He divided the Roman citizens into tribes and fixed the military obligations of five census-determined classes.
- **Tarquinius Superbus** (Tarquin the Proud; c. 534–510 BCE) was the last Etruscan king, as well as the last king of Rome. He was known for his cruelty, and his family acted outrageously in public. He was forcibly ousted by Brutus, who saw the Republic as more important than any single man. After being driven out, Tarquin tried to recapture Rome with the aid of the Etruscan king Lars Porsenna, but lost. Brutus and Collatinus emerged as the leaders of the new order in Rome. They believed Rome should be ruled by more than one person, leading to the rule of two consuls at the beginning of the Republic.

THE GEOGRAPHY OF ROME

Built on seven hills on the Tiber River, Rome was an advantageous place for a city. Its position on hills made it difficult for invaders to attack, and its access to water made it valuable for commerce as well as daily life. The construction of the city proceeded during the monarchy and continued into the Republic. Several physical landmarks still stand.

The forum, originally a marshy valley between the Quirinal and Esquiline Hills, became the focus of public and political life. It was divided down the middle by the *cloaca maxima*, probably originally meant to be a storm sewer or drainage ditch. By the 6th century BCE, it was covered, and by the 2nd century BCE, it was Rome's chief sewer. Shops and houses lined the forum on the northeast and southwest sides. People assembled in the *comitium*, a rectangular enclosure oriented to the four points of the compass. The Senate House (*curia*) was built into the north end of the *comitium*, as was a speaker's platform, the *rostra*. On the southeast end of the forum, a public meeting place, stood the *regia*, the former kings' palace. It was now occupied by the *pontifex maximus* ("greatest bridge maker" in Latin) and Vestal Virgins (women devoted to the worship of the goddess Vesta). The *pontifex maximus* was the head of the Roman priesthood and the ultimate authority on Roman religion in general. The office of Pope is a direct descendant from the office of the *pontifex maximus.* Vestal Virgins were chosen from young patrician girls who were 6–10 years old, and served the goddess for the next 40 years of their lives.

THE REPUBLIC

The Republic began with the expulsion of the last king, Tarquinius Superbus, and the rule by two consuls, which began as an interim form of government but would later become a permanent fixture in the Roman Republic. This second period of Roman history was marked by the presence of important leaders and conquests. The battles of this period were greater than any that followed in solidifying the reputation of Rome as powerful. Many famous names emerge in this period, but no leader of Rome ever enjoyed the military reputation of Julius Caesar, who was a master military strategist and political tactician. Caesar's crossing of the Rubicon signaled the end of the Republic and the beginning of rule by one supreme ruler again in the Western world.

THE CURSUS HONORUM

The Republic was created by and for patricians who had complete control over the plebeians (common people) and all slaves, with the exception of periodic rebellions to wrest power away to the common people. Executive power was given to two consuls or, as an alternative during times of crisis, one dictator who reigned supreme for a 6-month period. One prime example of that structure at work was the farmer Cincinnatus (Latin for "curly," referring to his hair), who became a dictator for 6 months during the war between the Romans and the Aequi and then returned to his farming, laying down the mantle of power.

In order to become a consul, however, a Roman leader usually had to work his way up the ladder, called the *cursus honorum* or "course of honors." First, Roman leaders had to complete 10 years of compulsory military service. After returning to Rome, the first office one had to hold was that of the *quaestor,* or treasurer, who oversaw the financial welfare of the state. After serving as *quaestor,* a politician could gain admission to the Roman senate. However, the next step on the ladder was the *aedile.* This official put on games to keep the public happy, from chariot races to gladiatorial fights. The term most associated with this office was *panem et circenses* or "bread and circuses." Romans believed that the lower classes of Rome would be kept happy as long as they had enough food and entertainment, and that was the aim of the *aedile*. The next step was the *praetor*, or the judge. These men would preside over criminal trials in Rome.

After completing each of these steps, a Roman man could theoretically be elected *consul*, as long as he was at least 39 years old. Some *consuls* notably skipped individual steps in the *cursus honorum*. Cicero, for example, never performed his military service. Nonetheless, the pathway to leadership was relatively well-defined for a Roman with political ambitions.

Over time, plebeians gained power within the governing structure by using the power of secession from the city as a weapon, as their manpower was needed to carry out the affairs of state, particularly in the arena of the military. They soon had their own tribunes in the senate who could introduce and enact laws. Yet the wealthy and the well-born continued to have enormous influence over the Roman state of affairs. Reforms, especially over new land and debts, kept the plebeians happy and the Romans united against enemies during this period.

IMPORTANT LEADERS

Marius and Sulla were two important rivals in the Republican period who ultimately shaped politics for generations to come. Marius was a popular general and politician who was elected *consul* seven times. He reformed the Roman military system and acted as general during a war in Numidia. Sulla, who originally served as Marius' *quaestor*, claimed credit for the end to the war in Numidia, and would later clash with Marius in a bloody civil war that divided all of Rome into two groups—the liberal *Populares* (who supported Marius) and the conservative *Optimates* (who supported Sulla). Even after the death of both men, the divisions into two camps or parties remained in Rome.

After the deaths of Marius and Sulla, the Republic was dominated by the first triumvirate, of which Caesar and his many military victories were central. Formed as an alliance to consolidate power in 60 BCE, the triumvirate possessed both military credentials and money to enhance its credibility although it had no formal power, only informal influence.

The first triumvirate was composed of Caesar, Pompey, and Crassus. The rise of Pompey was based on his military prowess abroad. Quashing Spartacus and the slave rebellion by Crassus qualified him for military fame as well as his money. Pompey became head of state at 36 and made himself the new Alexander. He and Caesar became rivals in the Roman

Civil War, with Caesar pursuing Pompey to Egypt, where Cleopatra's older brother had Pompey killed and his head placed in a wine jar. Later Caesar was declared dictator *perpetuus* (dictator for life), a move that led to the conspiracy to assassinate him, as there was a fear of a return to the rule of kings. A group of senators, including his friend Brutus, assassinated Caesar on the Ides of March (March 15th) in 44 BCE.

In the vacuum left after Caesar's death, the second triumvirate was formed, composed of Antony (the military man), Lepidus (the moneybags), and Octavian (the political man of family connections to Caesar). This joint rule lasted until Augustus was proclaimed emperor after the Battle of Actium, at which he defeated Antony and Cleopatra and cemented his leadership over Rome and its provinces, including Egypt.

THE ROMAN EMPIRE

Even though Rome enjoyed the rule of more than 100 emperors across the four centuries of the empire, there were specific groups of them worthy of commentary for their deeds and their character as leaders.

THE EMPERORS OF NOTE

Augustus was Rome's first emperor and best known today, due to his extensive building programs, his longevity in office (more than 40 years), his conquests of lands, his capacity to project his image on artistic works, and his patronage of great poets who paid homage to him in their lasting works. He also was an effective administrator who delegated responsibilities to able lieutenants who carried out his wishes in the provinces and at home in Rome. During his reign, Rome was at peace, prosperous, and united in a set social order internally. He expanded the empire and enriched it in many ways, from roads to monuments to water systems. He was named head of the state religion as well as the empire, thereby consolidating his power over all spheres of Roman life. Augustus was succeeded in office by his stepson **Tiberius** after the death of many other choices at an earlier stage.

The Julio-Claudian emperors (Augustus–Nero) represented the first stage of the empire; the name derives from the fact that they all were related either to Julius Caesar or Claudius.

The next emperors, after Augustus, were not so propitious. They included **Caligula,** perhaps the cruelest and most insane man to hold the office.

The disabled **Claudius** was effective and kind in the role, although he almost was not selected due to his disability and how such characteristics were viewed in the Roman empire at the time. He improved the civil service and extended citizenship during his rule. He was succeeded, however, by another miscreant, his stepson **Nero**, who was both cruel and vain.

Coming to power at age 17 and under the influence of his mother, Nero ordered executions and spent his time performing in song and lyre in the provinces, especially in Greece, and generally behaving erratically. During his reign, Rome experienced a great fire that destroyed important parts of the city, which he never rebuilt. He blamed the fire on the Christians and built a golden palace (the Domus Aurea) for himself over the ashes of the slums that had been destroyed. He ultimately was driven out and committed suicide in 68.

In the next period, the military again regained control over the politics and the fate of Rome. With **Vespasian**, the Romans acquired a successful commander as their emperor. He was responsible for establishing the **Flavian dynasty of emperors (Vespasian–Domitian)** which continued under his son **Titus** and his brother **Domitian**. They were mindful of providing for the army and under the short reign of Titus, his famous arch was erected along with the Colosseum. The terrible volcano eruption that buried both Pompeii and Herculaneum, the leisure estates of wealthy Romans, occurred during his reign.

The **Antonine emperors (Nerva–Marcus Aurelius)** gave imperial rule a moral basis, contending that the emperor was the best man for the job, a man of proven ability and integrity. Thus, the five good emperors ruled, beginning with **Nerva**, who chose **Trajan** as his successor. Trajan ruled for almost 20 years. He adopted an ambitious building program still seen today in a column named for him and invented the first shopping mall, known as the Trajan markets in Rome. The Senate awarded him the official title *Optimus Princeps* (Best of Leaders) to mark his favor.

Hadrian was Trajan's successor and also ruled for almost 20 years. His contributions ranged from administrative diligence to the building of Hadrian's Wall in northern Britain to defend against an attack from the Celts. He was well-liked by both the military and the provincial officials for his personal attention to problems, his energy, and his willingness to travel and be seen throughout the empire. His building program included

the Pantheon and a personal villa outside the city. **Antoninus Pius** succeeded Hadrian and ensured his predecessors' reputation by insisting on his deification. Again, the empire went through an uneventful but prosperous period.

The last of the good emperors was **Marcus Aurelius**, who was a Stoic philosopher as well as an emperor, ruling for another 20 years. Even though he had good intentions, he was faced with many battles that did not end well for Rome, and he violated the rule of prior good emperors by choosing his son Commodus as his successor, a decidedly poor choice. Commodus was vain, naming all the months after himself, and behaved like he was the hero Hercules even though he was a small man who was anything but dedicated to the public good.

Edward Gibbon, writing in the 18th century about Rome's decline, noted that

> If a man were called to fix the period in the history of the world, during which the condition of the human race was most happy and prosperous, he would, without hesitation, name that which elapsed from the death of Domitian to the accession of Commodus.

Thus the reputations of the five great emperors and their 80 years of reign were cemented for posterity by a historian several centuries removed from the events.

In the 3rd century BCE, Rome experienced many emperors and many crises of leadership along the way. **Valerian** was even captured by the Persians, an ignoble situation for the Romans to bear. **Claudius II** and **Aurelius** both restored military might and built defenses to protect the city (e.g., the Aurelian Wall).

Septimius Severus, an emperor who understood the important role of the army in maintaining power, was said to have rewarded his generals well for their loyalty and passed the advice on to his sons. For the most part they emulated him, although one, **Caracalla**, had his brother murdered for fear of usurpation. In turn, Caracalla was killed by his own army, suggesting his father was right in his view of the importance of the alliance with the military.

Diocletian, one of the important last emperors, devised a system called a tetrarchy (rule of four) to preserve imperial harmony by ensuring shared power over the vast Empire. The business of the empire was run by a dozen or so religious sectors and their vicars, setting up the ecclesiastical hierarchy that would survive into the Middle Ages. Two members of the tetrarchy were younger men who were mentored by the older pair to ready them for complete takeover of responsibility when the time came. Diocletian was an excellent role model for an emperor, voluntarily resigning his post after 21 years, a unique act in imperial Roman history although it harkens back to the earlier leadership view of Cincinnatus.

THE DECLINE AND FALL OF ROME

Rome suffered from several key defeats that weakened its stronghold as a world power. First of all, its army was comprised of as many barbarians—what the Romans called members of tribes outside Rome—as Romans, so the issue of loyalty was an internal concern. Secondly, the abandonment of Britain due to pressures in the East damaged the role of Rome in its provinces. The most serious attack, however, came on Rome itself by the Vandals in 410 AD and again in 455 when the imperial capital was moved to Milan. The Huns also invaded Roman territories and provinces with regularity and uneven results. These visible signs of weakness also took a psychological toll on the Roman citizens, leading to an acceptance of a passing era.

The eastern capital of Constantinople (new Rome), created during the reign of **Constantine**, survived and even thrived under **Justinian**'s rule during the 6th century. He was able to establish a code of law that remained influential in Western Europe for several centuries to come. He also instituted a building program of great prominence, marked by the construction of the Hagia Sophia in his capital city. Yet **Justinian's** rule was marred by an outbreak of the bubonic plague, which took his life. Afterward, his Byzantine empire was conquered by other Germanic tribes that ultimately held sway and erased—through neglect, not intent—much of the work of the Romans before.

Thus, the fall of Rome was more a slide into oblivion through lack of attention to aspects of societal infrastructure and functioning that were not seen as important by the barbarian tribes that gained control of the lands of the former Empire rather than a deliberate plan to dismantle what had made Rome work. Moreover, the last century also saw Rome do many things that hastened its demise—overexpansion of its territories, high taxes on its citizenry, and political unrest among various social classes. These internal problems also contributed to the demise of one of the greatest civilizations the world has ever known.

CONCLUSION

The history of Rome and its three stages of different types of government allow us to understand its evolution as a world power, the players who acted on its behalf as military leaders or civilian kings and emperors, and its important battles that were decisive in the expansion of a small land to one that commanded half the known world, ranging from Western to Eastern Europe and from North Africa to the Asian steppes. The Romans as builders, as military strategists, and as governors were nonpareil in capacity and scope of imagination.

Timeline From Rome's Founding to the End of the Augustan Age

753 BCE	The founding of Rome by Romulus and Remus
509 BCE	Downfall of monarchy and establishment of the Republic
264–241 BCE	First Punic War (war with Carthage)
218–201 BCE	Second Punic War
202 BCE	Defeat of Hannibal at the Battle of Zama, ending the Second Punic War
107 BCE	First Consulship of Marius
88 BCE	First Consulship of Sulla
73–71 BCE	Slave revolt and defeat of Spartacus
60–53 BCE	First triumvirate: Caesar, Pompey, and Crassus
49 BCE	Caesar crosses the Rubicon and conquers Rome
44 BCE	Assassination of Julius Caesar
43 BCE	Death of Cicero
43–33 BCE	Second triumvirate—Octavian, Lepidus, and Antony
31 BCE	Octavian defeats Antony and Cleopatra at Actium
29 BCE	Vergil starts work on the *Aeneid*
27 BCE	Octavian becomes Augustus; the Republic is restored

19 BCE	Death of Vergil
14 CE	Death of Augustus

Timeline of Selected Roman Emperors

27 BCE–14 CE	Augustus
14–37 CE	Tiberius
37–41 CE	Caligula
41–54 CE	Claudius
54–68 CE	Nero
69–79 CE	Vespasian
79–81 CE	Titus
81–96 CE	Domitian
96–98 CE	Nerva
98–117 CE	Trajan
117–138 CE	Hadrian
138–161 CE	Antoninus Pius
161–180 CE	Marcus Aurelius
177–192 CE	Commodus
193–211 CE	Septimius Severus
198–217 CE	Caracalla
253–260 CE	Valerian
268–270 CE	Claudius II
270–275 CE	Aurelian
285–305 CE	Diocletian
306–337 CE	Constantine the Great
475–476 CE	Romulus Augustus (last Roman emperor)

RESOURCES

Bowman, A., Cameron, A., & Garnse, G. (2005). *The Cambridge ancient history, Volumes 8–12* (2nd ed.). Cambridge, England: Cambridge University Press.

Forsythe, G. (2005). *A critical history of early Rome: From pre-history to the first Punic War*. Berkeley, CA: University of California Press.

Harris, N. (2000). History of ancient Rome. London, England: Octopus.

Hill, D. (2007). *Ancient Rome: From the Republic to the Empire*. Bath, England: Paragon Books.

Holland, T. (2003). *Rubicon, the triumph and tragedy of the Roman republic*. London, England: Abacus.

Lessing, E., & Varone, A. (1995). *Pompeii*. Paris, France: Bayard Presse S.A.

Shelton, J. (1998). *As the Romans did: A sourcebook in Roman social history*. Oxford, England: Oxford University Press.

Toynbee, A. (1972). *A study of history*. Oxford, England: Oxford University Press.

Wickham, C. (2009). *The inheritance of Rome*. London, England: Penguin.

CHAPTER 5

THE POWER OF WORDS

THE LITERATURE, RELIGION, AND PHILOSOPHY OF ANCIENT ROME

> *Auream quisquis mediocritatem diligit, tutus caret*
> *obsolete sordibus tecti, caret invidenda sobrius aula.*
> Whoever cultivates the golden mean avoids both the
> poverty of a hovel and the envy of a palace.
>
> —Horace

> Do not forget: A man needs little to lead a happy life.
>
> —Marcus Aurelius

INTRODUCTION

The Roman world of literature, religion, and philosophy is predominantly one inherited from the Greeks. The Romans retained the pagan religion of the Greeks but gave the gods and goddesses Romanized names even though they performed similar roles. The epic style of Homer was emulated by Vergil, and the philosophies of Stoicism and Epicureanism were passed on wholesale for Roman consumption. Yet the Romans built on and surpassed the Greeks in some of their literary products and interpretations of religion and philosophy.

When we consider the importance of words in any ancient culture, including the Roman one, we must remember how few of their words actually survive compared to the number they wrote. Only the classic *De Rerum Natura* (*On the Nature of Things,* a work of philosophy in poetic form) survives of Lucretius, for example. Of the 1,000 or so books written by the founders of Stoicism (Chrysippus) and Epicureanism (Epicurus), no original manuscripts survive. The great Greek dramatists also fared poorly in the survival of their prolific output. Only seven plays survive of Aeschylus and the same number for Sophocles, even though their written products exceeded 80 and 120 respectively. Writings of other well-known ancients have also been lost. Consequently, when we survey the contribution of Roman culture or other ancient ones, we do so with only partial evidence of their accomplishments.

WHERE HAVE ALL THE BOOKS GONE?

Due to climate, pests, and the demise of the intellectual tradition in places like Alexandria, Egypt, where the great library holdings at one time exceeded a half million papyrus rolls all carefully catalogued, ancient books in their original forms have disappeared. Even ancient libraries themselves have fallen victim to religious purges and natural disasters, never to be rebuilt. The Alexandrian Library in Egypt, which once burnt to the ground, is a notable exception, but the famous library at Pergamon, for example, is a pile of ruined and uneven stones punctuated by wild grasses.

THE SURVIVING LITERATURE OF ROME

The Romans were imitators of Greece's literary history as well as its visual arts. Seneca the Younger relied heavily on Sophocles and Euripides for his ideas about theatre. Plautus and Terence often copied plots and ideas straight out of the writings of the Greek Menander. Plautus in particular was viewed as a direct descendant of Aristophanes and his comedies. Even the great Latin epic *The Aeneid* derives many of its themes and elements from Homer's *Odyssey* and *Iliad*, between his use of the epic form and the wanderings of his uniquely Roman hero Aeneas.

ROMAN WRITERS OF DISTINCTION

Yet Roman writers and thinkers had their own originality, born of their particular experiences and the more generic ones of their culture. Vergil's *Aeneid* stands as the greatest piece of poetry composed to celebrate the founding of a society. As Aeneas leaves the burning city of Troy with his aged father Anchises on his back and his son Ascanius holding his hand, he sails into a sea of troubles in his quest to find Italy. Horace, the famous odist, celebrated the virtues of Roman character and culture in a succinct manner that allows him to remain among the best poets in that form. Plautus and Terence together brought a new comedic form into play in Roman culture, one that is arguably much funnier than their Greek source. Catullus invented a new kind of poetry that focused on the power of emotions. Ovid, in love with mythology, converted tales of human and godly transformations into riveting poetry.

THE PHILOSOPHIES OF ANCIENT ROME

Two of the most important philosophies in ancient Rome were Stoicism and Epicureanism. The Stoic school of thought held that wisdom lies in mastering our passions and reordering our desires to want what is morally good. This philosophy is demonstrated in Vergil's *Aeneid*, in which the hero continues on his journey to found Rome and follow the will of the gods in spite of the destruction of his home city of Troy. Epicurean philosophy was named for the writer Epicurus, whose ideas are captured in the Latin phrase *"carpe diem"* (seize the day). Epicurus and his followers held that once we accept that the soul dies with the body, we will be relieved from anxieties about what will happen after death and can focus on enjoying the pleasures that this world has to offer. Perhaps this philosophy is best articulated in the great work *De Rerum Natura* (frequently translated as *On the Nature of the Things*), a poetic treatise by Lucretius. According to Steven Greenblatt, author of *The Swerve: How the World Became Modern*, Lucretius thought that

> What human beings can and should do is to conquer their fears, accept the fact that they themselves and all the things they encounter are transitory, and embrace the beauty and pleasure of the world. (p. 6)

The notion of atoms goes back to 5th century Greece, yet it was Lucretius who best articulated its tenets. Atoms were seen as the building blocks of life, small in size and numerous, that were responsible for the creation of all life forms. They operated according to universal principles that man could grasp and take pleasure in knowing. Matter was always in motion, and only random collision brought about significant change in how the world worked.

What makes the Lucretius poem unique in literature is its reasoned system of philosophy, written in verse. The title *De Rerum Natura* implies the importance of scientific concerns over artistic ones, the primacy of the content over the processes of language used to create it. Like most of Rome's poets, Lucretius used dactylic hexameter, a Greek meter common in Latin poetry, to compose his greatest work, which was probably published posthumously (*post* = after and *humus* = Earth; literally, after he was buried).

A contemporary of Lucretius was Catullus, perhaps the greatest lyric poet of Rome. Writing for a brief period of time, he crafted some 114 separate poems, some about his unrequited love for a woman he calls Lesbia, some about social mores of the time, and some invective (*in* = against and *vect* = carried; literally, a speech attacking someone) against his enemies. His most famous phrase "*Odi et amo*" (I hate and I love) captures the deeply personal nature of Catullus and his poetry. Like many famous lovelorn poets (the English lyric poet Keats comes to mind), he died young, at age 30 in the first century BCE.

The second era of Roman poets included both Vergil and Horace. Both capitalized on the work that had gone before but brought new and deeper insights into what it meant to be Roman. This golden age of Roman poetry also included the work of Ovid, who was fascinated by mythology and transferred that fascination to his poetry.

ROMAN PAGANISM

The Romans were polytheistic, believing in many gods who controlled the workings of their universe. They also were often called pantheistic (*pan* = all; *theos* = gods; literally, worshipping all the gods) because of the pervasive (*per* = through and *vado* = go; literally, goes through) presence of their gods in animating nature. They anthropomorphized (*anthropos* = man and *morphos* = change; literally changed into man) the basic elements of nature—like fire, water, and wind—and created myths to explain natural events like the rising and setting of the sun each day, the quality of trees and flowers, and even the defining characteristics of insects. They also created heroic myths that explained how mortal men could behave in godlike ways in order to accomplish difficult tasks and acquire fame and fortune in their lifetimes. This belief system also penetrated the art and literature of the Romans, providing a written and visual language of expression of basic human needs, wants, and emotions.

The Romans also personalized worship to the local gods in the home, which was more based on their origins as a people. The *penates,* worshipped by Romans on a hearth or shrine in the home, symbolized the ancient gods brought by Aeneas from Troy, while the *lares* symbolized the gods of the Latium region they now inhabited. In the Roman temple, the *pontifex maximus* consulted oracles and read augurs (the flight of birds) as well as inspected the form of sacrificial animal victims to uncover the future and guide human behavior. The wife of Caesar, for example, was purported to have told him not to go to the Senate on the ides (15th) of March because a soothsayer in the temple had said that an ill omen suggested it was dangerous for him to do so. Portents, omens, sacrifices, and the motions of birds in the sky all shaped Roman belief, and as a result, Roman history.

THE POWER OF MYTH

The Olympian gods and goddesses, a Greek invention, were also adopted by the Romans along with their many associated myths. The Romans derived much of their mythology through oral tradition from the Greeks, but they changed the names.

The 12 main gods and goddesses, who are all related, include:

- **Zeus** (Roman name: Jupiter): The god of the sky and the king of Olympus. His moods affected the weather, and he threw thunderbolts when he was unhappy. He was married to Hera but had relationships with many other women. His symbols include the oak, the eagle, and the thunderbolt.
- **Hera** (Roman name: Juno): The goddess of marriage and the queen of Olympus. She was Zeus's wife and sister; many myths tell of how she sought revenge when Zeus betrayed her with his

lovers. Her symbols include the peacock (which she created) and the cow.

- **Poseidon** (Roman name: Neptune): The god of the sea. He was the most powerful god except for his brother, Zeus. He lived alone in a palace under the sea and caused earthquakes when he was in a foul mood. His symbols include the horse (which he created) and the trident, a three-pronged spear.

- **Hades** (Roman name: Pluto): King of the dead. He lived in the Underworld, the heavily guarded land where he ruled over the dead. He was the brother of Zeus and the husband of young Persephone (Proserpina in Latin) whom he kidnapped. (You can read the full myth in the Time unit.)

- **Aphrodite** (Roman name: Venus): The goddess of love and beauty and the protector of sailors. She may have been the daughter of Zeus and the Titaness Dione, or she may have arisen from sea foam, often depicted on a shell. Her symbols include the myrtle tree and the dove.

- **Apollo** (Roman name: Apollo): The god of music, poetry, and healing. He was also an archer, and hunted with a silver bow. Apollo was the son of Zeus and the Titaness Leto and the twin of Artemis. His symbols include the laurel tree, the crow, and the dolphin.

- **Ares** (Roman name: Mars): The god of war. Ares was the son of Zeus and Hera, but neither of his parents liked him. He was seen as cruel in his interactions with mortals and even the other gods. In spite of being the god of war, he is often depicted as a coward. His symbols include the vulture and the dog, and he often carried a bloody spear.

- **Artemis** (Roman name: Diana): The goddess of the hunt and the protector of women in childbirth. She hunted with silver arrows and loved all wild animals. Artemis was the daughter of Zeus and Leto, and the twin of Apollo. Her symbols include the cypress tree and the deer.

- **Athena** (Roman name: Minerva): The goddess of wisdom. She was also skilled in the art of war and helped heroes such as Odysseus and Hercules. Athena sprang full-grown from the forehead of Zeus—he had a headache, asked Hephaestus to split his head open, and out she sprang in adult form and clothed in armor. She soon became his favorite child. Her symbols include the owl and the olive tree (which she created). She is often depicted with a helmet and a shield with the head of Medusa on it.

- **Hephaestus** (Roman name: Vulcan): The god of fire and the forge. Although he made armor and weapons for the gods, he loved peace. Often depicted as lame and ugly, he was the son of Zeus and Hera and married Aphrodite. His symbols include the anvil and the forge. The word "volcano" derives from his name.
- **Hestia** (Roman name: Vesta): The goddess of the hearth. She was the most gentle of the gods, and does not play a role in many myths. Hestia was the sister of Zeus and the oldest of the Olympians. Fire is among her symbols. She was the basis for the Vestal Virgins, the nine women who guarded and tended the temple fire in Rome.
- **Hermes** (Roman name: Mercury): The messenger god, a trickster, and a friend to thieves. He was said to have invented boxing and gymnastics. He was the son of Zeus and Maia. The speediest of all, he wore winged sandals and a winged hat and carried a magic wand.

These deities remain above the human race but also interact with it in times of trouble. Humans make mistakes and often offend the gods and are punished by them as a result. When men take on too much power or authority or belief in their own abilities, the gods prescribe a punishment fitting to the crime.

THE BELIEF IN FATE

Just as the Romans believed in pagan gods and created stories to explain their powers in nature, so too they believed in fate. As with the gods, they anthropomorphized the process of life and death. The life of every person was predestined by the work of the three fates—Clotho, Lachesis, and Atropos. These three sisters controlled human existence from birth to death. Clotho wove the thread of life, Lachesis spun it out, and Atropos, with her dread scissors, cut it off. Thus, the belief system of the Romans included humanlike figures as explanation for all that befell them, from natural circumstance to the basic span of years they enjoyed.

THE MYTHIC HERO

The most popular myths involve major heroes—Aeneas, Theseus, Jason, Perseus, Hercules. These heroes undertake a journey, seek a reward, and come to understand

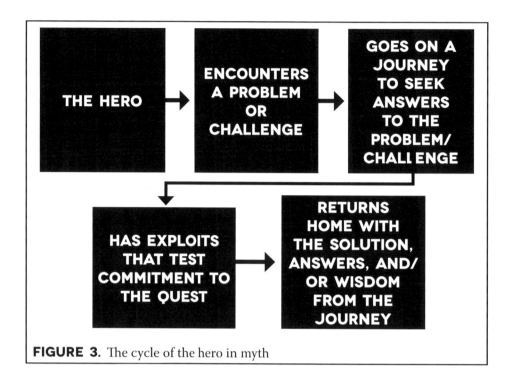

FIGURE 3. The cycle of the hero in myth

the consequences of persistence toward a goal. They return with new insights, treasure, and power, and must deal with the realities of life without the adventure of the unknown. The heroic cycle may be characterized by Figure 3.

Other powerful myths involve humans exhibiting hubris (i.e., excessive pride) that displeases the gods, who often convert the offending mortal into another creature out of pity or anger. Arachne is transformed into a spider for her pride in weaving that challenges Athena. Sometimes the gods pity mortals for their foibles. Clytie is changed to a sunflower because of her love for Apollo, the sun god, as he crosses the skies. Sometimes the gods inflict punishment out of jealousy. Hera is frequently depicted punishing any of Zeus' many lovers, or the offspring of those unions. For example, she torments Hercules as a son of Zeus and a mortal woman, just as she does many other heroes. Other times, the gods reward humans for faithful behavior in their service. In another myth, the old married couple Baucis and Philemon show hospitality to Zeus and Hermes, and the gods turn them into an oak and a linden tree so that they can stay together forever. The youth Narcissus becomes a flower who can forever gaze at his visage in the water. All of these myths contain powerful morals about human behavior.

Then we have myths that explain natural phenomena controlled by the gods. Apollo rides his sun chariot across the sky to explain the rising and setting of the sun. Poseidon stirs up the seas out of anger, causing shipwrecks. The wind gods blow their forceful breath, causing havoc or good fortune to ships and humans alike. Ares exercises his warlike qualities to demonstrate how conflict occurs in human situations. Aphrodite and her son Eros strike humans with the feeling of love and cause both pleasure and misery as a result.

CONCLUSION

The legacy of ideas in the form of philosophy, religion, and literature creates a cross-cutting effect in Roman civilization. The literature of myth becomes the greatest poetry of the Romans under Ovid's skilled hand. The philosophy of Epicureanism and Stoicism come alive in the poetic works of Lucretius and Vergil. The religious paganism of gods and goddesses flourishes in both the literary and visual arts of ancient Rome. We have only to consult the common saying from the culture—*Ars longa vita brevis* (Art is long, life is short)—to realize the power of these ideas encased in the Latin language and fed by ancient beliefs.

REFERENCES AND RESOURCES

Boorstin, D. J. (1998). *The seekers*. New York, NY: Vintage.

Bulfinch, T. (1979). *Bulfinch's mythology*. New York, NY: Gramercy.

Greenblatt, S. (2011). *The swerve: How the world became modern*. New York, NY: Norton.

Hamilton, E. (1981). *Mythology*. Toronto, ON: Penguin.

Rodgers, N. (2008). *Ancient Rome*. Leicester, England: Hermes House.

CHAPTER 6

REMNANTS OF THE PAST
ROMAN ART AND ARCHITECTURE

> *Ars longa vita brevis*
> Art endures while life is short.

> Great nations write their autobiographies in three manuscripts, the book of their deeds, the book of their words, and the book of their art. Not one of these books can be understood unless we read the two others, but of the three, the only trustworthy one is the last.
> —John Ruskin, 19th-century English essayist

INTRODUCTION

In studies of the ancient world, it is a common idea that Romans were copyists more than original creators when it came to artistic enterprises. Whether considering the great architecture or sculpture or decorations of the ancients, we often acknowledge Greek models as the definitive ones—for example, the Doric, Ionic, and Corinthian columns were created by the Greeks and used by the Romans with little alteration. Roman classical sculptures of mythological figures depicted in three-dimensional form also appear very similar to Greek examples.

Yet the Romans were clearly original in their ability to apply artistic features for practical use. In that sense, they were innovators, taking the best from the past and employing it in a new way to serve a purpose for improvement of the society. Their engineering feat of arches and bridges has never been equaled in scale or utility. Their wall paintings, used as internal home decoration in Pompeii and Herculaneum, are unique, as are the mosaics used as flooring for wealthy homes. In the first century CE, they helped to define the Hellenistic (*Hellas* = Greek) period of art as they conquered Greek-influenced countries and served as important patrons of the continuing evolution of classical art.

In addition to being influenced and even entranced by the art of the Greeks, the Romans also incorporated many artistic ideals from their former conquerors and Italian neighbors, the Etruscans.

Much of their early art (circa 500–100 BCE) was basically Etruscan, revealing the archaic style of one-dimensionality. The art that remains of the Etruscans is primarily small bronze statuary and funerary sarcophagi (stone coffins with ornate decoration). These art objects attest to a lively culture that valued family, respected deities, and worshipped the fantastic in the form of creatures that had combined traits, sometimes of humans and sometimes multiple animals. The chimaera, for example, was a lion with a head of a goat arising out of the back of the creature and a snake's tail.

ROMAN ARTISTIC EXAMPLES

Two very famous pieces survive from the Hellenistic period. One is the single figure of *Victory*, found on the island of Samothrace and erected to commemorate a naval victory in 200 BCE. Now standing in the Louvre in Paris, the sculpture demonstrates the synthesis of movement and drapery, rarely done well in sculpture up to this time. A second fine example from the 1st century BCE is the group sculpture of

Laocoön and His Two Sons, called by Pliny the Elder the finest sculpture of antiquity, a claim that many have echoed through the ages. This piece, done by Rhodes sculptors, stands in the Vatican Museums in Rome.

To many art historians, the first great sculpted monument of the Imperial Age is the *Ara Pacis*, erected in Rome circa 13 BCE, to commemorate the establishment of peace in the Roman world (*Pax Romana*). It reflects the various stylistic harmonies of the Hellenistic period, from the use of mythology to depictions of nature to human models of distinguished Romans. It also represents the beginnings of historical events captured in relief sculpture.

THE GREATEST ROMAN ARTISTIC CONTRIBUTION

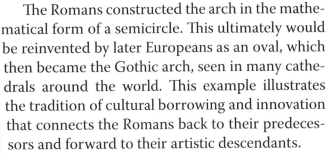

Perhaps the Romans' greatest contribution to Western civilization was their use of the arch for engineering purposes. This innovation contributed to another important one—the building of aqueducts (*aqua* = water, *duct* = lead) that carried water across obstacles to cities throughout the empire. Seen as a practical engineering invention by a culture more pragmatic than their architectural forebears—the Greeks and the Incans (Bronowski, 1973), the arch, in separate blocks of stone, represents the intellectual method of "splitting" nature apart and putting it together in new and more effective combinations.

The Romans constructed the arch in the mathematical form of a semicircle. This ultimately would be reinvented by later Europeans as an oval, which then became the Gothic arch, seen in many cathedrals around the world. This example illustrates the tradition of cultural borrowing and innovation that connects the Romans back to their predecessors and forward to their artistic descendants.

Although Assyrians created the first aqueduct to transport water to their capital city of Nineveh, Romans created a unique form for water transportation based on their arch to create a more stable structure. One of the best preserved aqueducts from the Roman period is the Pont du Gard near the French city of Arles. Another example of a fine aqueduct can be found in the gargantuan glory of the Segovian aqueduct in Spain, which spans a half-mile of more than 100 double-tiered arches. Totally intact, one can see the workmanship of the Romans in their desire to provide a pragmatic answer to sustaining the life of those in the provinces, or alternatively, allowing the citizens of Rome to enjoy luxurious fountains and public baths.

Public bathing was big business in ancient Rome, and existed in two forms. *Balneae* were small-scale bath houses, but *thermae* were large public complexes, with various rooms and pools, from the *apodyterium* (changing room) to the *palaestra* (exercise area) to the *tepidarium* (warm baths) to the *caldarium* (hot baths) to the *frigidarium* (cold baths). The Baths of Caracalla, also located in Rome, represented one such imperial structure, built to accommodate 1600 bathers at a time. This building was one of many built on such a grand scale in ancient Rome.

STRUCTURAL SCALE

The use of large-scale structures was also a feature of Roman edifices (*aedificium*, Latin for building), perhaps the best example being the Colosseum, built to house animals and the gladiators who would combat them. It could also be filled with water to host *naumachia*, large-scale mock naval battles. The columns and arches built to honor emperors also belong to this category of outsized artifacts. Trajan's column, located in the forum in Rome, is a prime example. The Arch of Titus also ranks high on the list of big building projects.

The most famous building that represents both scale and the spatial shape of a dome is the Pantheon (*pan* = all and *theos* = gods; literally a place to worship all the gods of Rome), an amalgam of Greek and Roman styles. This building pays homage to the religious appetites of the Romans by honoring the ancient gods at one site, and later served as a final resting place for Rome's elite.

ETERNAL FORMS

Bronze and marble were the preferred tools of the Romans for their sculpture. Often mimicking the Greek Hellenistic style, they favored the subject matter of the gods and great men. However, the beautiful idealized style eventually evolved into a unique Roman realism in which artists depicted figures as real individuals, warts and all, not as perfect models. This was an important development, as their household gods (i.e., the Lares and Penates) were made in the image of real ancestors of the family and stood as an altar to Roman realism in everyday art. Funerary art in the form of sarcophagi provide evidence of Greek and

Etruscan influence on Roman art and further elaborate myth and history. The lid of the sarcophagus often depicted the dead in a reclining pose, reminiscent of Etruscan vessels crafted for the same purpose. *Stelae* or stone relief sculptures used individual features of the deceased to depict likeness in life.

Some statues of Rome's great leaders retain a realistic air even as they seek to promote the greatness of Rome. Some statues weren't so lifelike, however. The Emperor Augustus preferred idealized forms for propaganda purposes. Whenever possible, artists depicted him in monumental size statuary in a commanding position of power. As popular as Augustus and his brokered Pax Romana was in his own time, his own propaganda pieces survive because of their idealized forms that were easily confused with other imperial statues. One of the most famous surviving bronzes of the emperor Augustus on horseback supposedly remains because he was mistaken for Constantine, who was revered in the next stage of history—so much for realistic depiction!

However, under Augustus, the style of Roman statuary changed. It now took on a larger purpose, one of proclaiming the godlike qualities of Rome's leaders, both former and current. Julius Caesar was also portrayed as a larger-than-life leader. In the posthumous work "the green Caesar," he is depicted as all-knowing and all-seeing in a bust of impressive size to commemorate his power and authority during his lifetime. His adopted heir benefitted from this image, and made sure his image would endure. As seen in the British Museum on the head of Augustus statue, the sheer power and assuredness of the gaze leaves no doubt about the leadership of Augustus over much of the known world. His ability to shape his image in art form and retain that image over time represents one of the great examples of human iconography.

ROMAN PAINTING

Most Roman painting that survives decorated the walls of houses in Pompeii and elsewhere that wealthy Romans lived or had summer villas. These wall paintings are known for several special features—their lavishness, their use of myth, and their love of nature. The materials used to create them also attest to the Roman fondness for color, especially the deep purples and rich, Pompeian red. Modern science, however, now reveals that the intense red color may have been a side effect of the gases released by Mount Vesuvius and that the original color used in so many houses in Pompeii was ochre.

Tarquinia, a city north of Rome, also has preserved wall paintings that reflect Roman mythology, the fondness for animal figures, and decorative patterns of various types.

Roman Egypt, established in 30 BCE and held by the Romans until 390 CE, came into Roman hands after the battle of Actium and the defeat of Antony by Octavian. Here encaustic paintings survive depicting realistic portraits of Romans now deceased. These portraits appear to be realistic and vivid, often painted on wood and buried with the mummified corpse, showing the combination of Egyptian and Roman styles.

MOSAICS

Perhaps the most prevalent example of Roman art found today is the mosaic, which has survived due to the durability of the materials in the face of variations in climate and temperature. Originally a Greek art form, the forming of black and white tesserae patterns became quite popular in Rome and spread from there to the provinces and North Africa, where color was more commonly used. Although often used to cover whole floors in Roman houses or atria, mosaics were also done as wall decoration.

FROM REALISM TO SYMBOLISM

In late antiquity (i.e., 5th century and onward), the use of realism in Roman art gives way to more symbolism to convey meaning. With the advent of Christianity, the use of symbols, such as the cross, the fish, and chi rho, becomes an important part of the human story. Roman sarcophagi such as the *Ludovisi Battle* (290 CE) depict a Roman general triumphantly going on to a better place after death, hinting at the Christian theme of the afterlife. Yet naturalistic detail and depiction of myth continues in many artistic works of the Romans for some time to come.

CONCLUSION

The legacy of Roman art may be seen in the great works of the Renaissance and beyond. Roman statues were copied and emulated. Donatello, the great Florentine sculptor, modeled his David after the sculpture of Antinous, the much-portrayed friend of the Emperor Hadrian. The Laocoön sculpture mentioned earlier helped shape the art of Michelangelo and others. Yet Roman art was not a celebration of individual artists, but rather a continuity in classical artistic traditions, both Greek and Etruscan, that influenced all of Europe and beyond for centuries.

REFERENCES AND RESOURCES

Bronowski, J. (1973). *Ascent of man.* Boston, MA: Little, Brown.

Clark, K. (1969). *Civilization.* New York, NY: Harper & Row.

Gowing, L. (1995). *A history of art.* New York, NY: Barnes & Noble.

Harris, N. (2000). *History of ancient Rome.* London, England: Octopus.

MacGregor, N. (2010). *A history of the world in 100 objects.* New York, NY: Viking.

Strong, D. (1965). *The classical world.* New York, NY: McGraw Hill.

PART II
UNITS OF STUDY

UNIT 1
TIME

> *Tempus fugit.*
> Time flies.
> —Common Latin motto

> *Sed fugit interea fugit irreparabile tempus, singula*
> *dum capti circumvectamur amore.*
> But meanwhile it flees, time flees, unrecoverable, while we
> are carried from place to place, captives of a love of detail.
> —Vergil, Georgics

CONCEPT OF TIME

The measurement of time in any culture is likely to show much of how that civilization considers its world and its place inside of it. Scientific measurement and superstition can be applied to the passing of the seasons in equal measure, and that mixture tells us much about the Romans. Religious festivals and naming customs for the months and days that made up their calendar indicate their belief in divinities that may or may not tend to their needs. At the same time, their system of lunar and solar cycles with *intercalares* (days added in to make the years a full 365 days), and their different forms of timekeeping and time measurement in different stages of Rome's development, reveal a society still growing up in the world. Rome struggled to find a balance between scientific evidence, superstition, and deference to rulers' definitions of the calendar from the very beginning of the monarchy through the end of empire. As difficult as they found it to create an effective calendar, they have had an immense impact on how we measure time today, both in nomenclature (naming) and enumeration (numbering).

KEY GENERALIZATIONS

» Time and how it is measured give an insight into the way Roman society is organized.
» Time chronicles significant events and people within Roman society via timelines of history.
» Time shows how the evolution of ideas about government, ethics and philosophy within Roman culture parallel those in other civilizations.
» Time provides structure and regulation to Roman life.

ESSENTIAL QUESTIONS

» How do the Romans measure time and what has been the Roman legacy in measuring time?
» How do Roman myths illustrate the concept of time?
» What eras or time periods of Roman history provide an understanding of the development and decline of this culture?
» How is the concept of time a basic metric for human understanding of the world?

GOALS AND OUTCOMES

» Develop an understanding of Roman metrics for time through the study of measurement and applications.

Students will be able to:
- create timelines illustrating the role of people and events in history, and
- analyze ancient and modern methods of time-keeping and what they reveal about a culture.

» Develop an understanding of key concepts that underlie Roman civilization.

Students will be able to:
- develop relevant products that apply the Roman concept of time, and
- evaluate ancient beliefs about time and associated concepts.

» Develop critical thinking and reasoning.

Students will be able to:
- evaluate the contribution of Roman innovations in time-keeping and calendars to other cultures,
- debate arguments to support the importance of selected events in Roman history, and
- analyze the major contributions of famous Romans across eras.

» Express creative ideas in multiple forms.

Students will be able to:
- create written and visual products that express ideas about key concepts, and
- synthesize multiple forms to create a timeline of Roman contributions.

LESSON 1

HOW DID THEY COUNT?

Instructional Purpose: To engage students in interdisciplinary thinking about math concepts.

Before students can study how Romans measured anything, they must first understand how a Roman would count. Appendix A in the back of the book contains a chart of important Roman numbers and numerals. In this lesson, students will examine Roman numbers and numerals from mathematical, practical, and cultural perspectives.

ACTIVITIES:

1. Group students into pairs to read through the list of Roman numerals included within Appendix A. Ask them to respond to the following questions.
   a. What mathematical patterns do you see in the way Romans wrote out numbers?
   b. What significance seems to come from placing a smaller number to the right of a larger number? A larger number next to a smaller number?
   c. Do they seem to use our concept of "places"—the ones place, the tens place, etc.?
   d. List the ways this system of numbers differs from our decimal system of Arabic numbers.

2. Pass out Handout 1.1: Roman Numerals as Hand Signals and have students practice communicating with hand signals to tell each other their age, the hour of the day, and the period of the day.
3. Discuss why the Romans may have chosen numerals that could be interpreted into hand signals. What does this say about Roman society and particularly, literacy?
4. Assign students in small groups to research another culture's system of counting. Assign one group ancient Mayan counting (base-20 numeral system), one group ancient Chinese counting (abacus), and one group Egyptian number systems.

5. Ask students to compare the number systems with the Roman system, making sure to include the following elements in their comparison: the base, symbols used for numbers, part-to-whole relationships (fractions, decimals), and concept of zero.

6. Ask groups to report their findings and discuss the similarities and differences across the numeric systems.

7. Have students individually journal on the following prompt: Speculate why different cultures came up with completely different number systems.

NAME: _____ **DATE:** _____

HANDOUT 1.1
ROMAN NUMERALS AS HAND SIGNALS

Many scholars believe that Roman numerals came from hand signals that allowed people of the Roman Empire to communicate, whatever their language or literacy level. Alfred Hooper, a scholar in the 20th century, was the first person to propose this idea in his 1945 book, *The River Mathematics.* According to his theory, the numbers I, II, and III correspond to the number of fingers held up to order something. V then represents the hand with fingers together and thumb apart. X would result from either crossing thumbs, or holding up both hands in an X-shape.

I = 1 finger
II = 2 fingers
III = 3 fingers
IV = 1 finger right hand, V on the left
V = V on the left hand
VI = V on the right hand, 1 on the left
VII = V on the right hand, 2 on the left
VIII = V on the right hand, 3 on the left
X = hold hands up in a cross

© Prufrock Press Inc. • *Ancient Roots and Ruins*

LESSON 2

VOCABULARY

Instructional Purpose: To engage students in connecting English vocabulary to Latin roots and stems.

Ninety percent of English words that have three or more syllables come from Latin. These words are derivatives because they are derived from Latin. Students will look for words that share similar letters and similar meanings to Latin words in this activity and see how many derivatives they can find. For example: *unus* means one in Latin; a **un**icorn has one horn; they share the letters "un"; therefore "unicorn" is a derivative of "*unus.*" Although the word "uncle" shares the letters "un," the word has nothing to do with the number one, so it is not a derivative. In this lesson, students will explore the world of derivatives from Latin.

ACTIVITIES:

1. Ask students to look at the same list of numbers, but now generate a list of derivatives, or words with similar meaning that share letters with the Latin words for each of these numbers (e.g., unicorn for *unus*). Students may want to use dictionaries for this activity. They should create a list of at least 20 derivatives in English from numbers 1–10.
2. Next, compose a paragraph that uses at least five of the original words.
3. Ask students to share their paragraphs in small groups.
4. What were favorite English words that students uncovered? Are there any words that the students are uncertain about? Share and discuss.
5. Have students research any "uncertain" derivatives using the Online Etymology Dictionary (http://www.etymonline.com)— they must present orally both the origin of the word and an explanation of why it is or is not related to their original number word.

LESSON 3

GRAMMAR AND USAGE

Instructional Purpose: To engage students with the Latin language and practice using vocabulary in context.

Students must learn basic phrases for communicating about time and time-keeping. The one question we ask the most in the modern day is "What time is it?" To answer both questions, students must know their numbers and their numerals.

The question "What time is it?" translates to "How many hours is it?" In Latin, "*Quota hora est?*" However, the answer depended very much on the number of hours from sunrise, since the Romans thought of their day as divided into light hours and dark hours, before and after the "meridiem" or noon-time, when the sun was highest in the sky. They invented the terms a.m. (ante meridiem or before noon) and p.m. (post meridiem or after noon).

Therefore to the question "*Quota hora est?*" a student could answer "*Quinta hora est post meridiem*" if it is between 4 p.m. and 5 p.m. (remember Roman inclusive counting—12 p.m. counts as the first hour after noon, 1 p.m. is the second, etc.) In this lesson, you will learn to tell the time in Latin, both aloud and in writing.

ACTIVITIES:

1. Now, have students review the numbers again, and guess what form the ordinal numbers (first, second, third, fourth, etc.) will be for those numbers, based on the example of *quinta*.
2. Ask them to compare their lists to Handout 3.1: Ordinal Numbers. Which ones were the same or similar, which ones were different?
3. Ask students why *quinta* ends with an "a" when there are multiple possible endings, such as *quintus* or *quintum*. Explain that every noun in Latin has a gender—feminine, masculine, or neuter. The word for hour is feminine, so the adjective that describes it must also be feminine.
4. Ask students to look up these same words in each of the Romance languages (French, Italian, Portuguese, Romanian, Spanish) using online dictionaries and tools such as Google Translate. Then

ask them to discuss how similar the words are and what letters changed significantly between the different languages.

5. Now, ask students to list the hours of daylight as a Roman would have, in both a.m. and p.m. See Handout 3.2: Timekeeping Key.

OPTIONAL EXTENSION

If students are interested, they may choose to create their own sundial as an extension. Keep in mind that this would represent a daylong commitment, since students must research the shadows cast by the sun during the course of a full day's worth of sunshine. Instructions can be found at eHow (http://www.ehow.com/how_4841694_sundials-kids.html).

HANDOUT 3.1

ORDINAL NUMBERS

	Masculine	**Feminine**	**Neuter**
First	Primus	Prima	Primum
Second	Secundus	Secunda	Secundum
Third	Tertius	Tertia	Tertium
Fourth	Quartus	Quarta	Quartum
Fifth	Quintus	Quinta	Quintum
Sixth	Sextus	Sexta	Sextum
Seventh	Septimus	Septima	Septimum
Eighth	Octavus	Octava	Octavum
Ninth	Nonus	Nona	Nonum
Tenth	Decimus	Decima	Decimum

© Prufrock Press Inc. • *Ancient Roots and Ruins*

HANDOUT 3.2

TIME-KEEPING KEY

Prague Castle, Prague, Czech Republic

Admiralty Arch, London, England

Modern Time-keeping
Sunrise

Ancient Time-keeping
1 a.m. = prima hora ante meridiem

The hour of this may vary, but this list assumes 6 a.m.

Modern	Ancient
7 a.m.	2 a.m. = secunda hora ante meridiem
8 a.m.	3 a.m.
9 a.m.	4 a.m.
10 a.m.	5 a.m.
11 a.m.	6 a.m.
12 p.m.	1 p.m.
1 p.m.	2 p.m.
2 p.m.	3 p.m.
3 p.m.	4 p.m.
4 p.m.	5 p.m.
5 p.m.	6 p.m.
6 p.m.	7 p.m.
7 p.m.	8 p.m.

LESSON 4

YEARS IN ROMAN NUMERALS

Instructional Purpose: To connect ancient and modern uses of Roman numerals.

Romans measured years in different ways according to the time period in the development of the Roman state. Each of these different metrics shows the popular values of the time and makes a different statement about Roman culture. In this lesson, you will learn ancient measures of time and examine modern monuments and how they use Roman numerals.

ACTIVITIES:

1. Before reading the provided handouts, ask students to discuss the units we use to measure time in the modern day. How are eras or centuries measured? Years? Months? Weeks? Days? Hours? Why do we break them up into these units? Why 7 days a week, for example? Is it all based on scientific fact?

2. Read Handout 4.1: The Roman Calendar and the website Virtual Roma (http://roma.andreapollett.com/S7/roma-cal.htm), then compare the Roman system to another ancient system of time measurement, the Mayan calendar. Consult this Prezi (http://prezi.com/kdpymtr6x4lp/the-rational-persons-guide-to-the-mayan-apocalypse/), then complete a Venn diagram comparing and contrasting the two.

3. More recent monuments also use Roman numerals in inscriptions, such as the two pictured in Handout 3.2: Timekeeping Key. Both of these are taken from more recent monuments, so their years are written in CE format. Have students examine the two inscriptions and answer the following questions.
   a. In what year was this monument built? Use your knowledge of Roman numerals. Research the specific monument online, for both the purpose of the building and the general history around when it was built.
   b. Why would the architect(s) have chosen to include Roman numerals and Latin in the inscription at this stage of history

in this part of the world? Are the Romans and their culture particularly relevant to the purpose of these buildings? Look up at least two other monuments that use Roman numerals and justify the architect's decision to include Roman numerals and/or Latin.

HANDOUT 4.1
THE ROMAN CALENDAR

Romans measured years in different ways according to the time period in the development of the Roman state. At the start of the monarchy, under the reign of Romulus, the calendar was made up of lunar cycles and seasons, and only had 295 days, as they chose not to count those days in the winter when Romans could not work the land in the field. The second king of Rome, Numa Pompilius, brought the number of days on Rome's official calendar up to 355, adding in *intercalares* where necessary to account for the difference. It took three more reformations of the calendar before Augustus, the first emperor of Rome, reformed the calendar into 365.25 days. Not until Pope Gregory XIII reformed the calendar again in 1582 did the calendar as we know it (with an accurate number of days) take shape.

Today, we mark our years of 365 days (with a leap year every 4 years) according to BC (Before Christ) and AD (*Anno Domini*, Latin for "in the year of our Lord"), or alternatively BCE (Before Common Era) and CE (Common Era). In the time of the Republic, they often did not specify a numeric year, preferring instead to name the consuls from that year. However, if they had to give the year as a number, as on a monumental inscription, they used the traditional date of Rome's founding—April 21st, 753 BCE. This was marked as AUC, which stood for *ab urbe condita* (Latin for "from the founding of the city").

To understand how to read Roman inscriptions of time, you must first understand how the Romans counted. The first rule to know about Roman numbers is that Romans had an inclusive counting system. Therefore, if this year is 2013 CE and Rome was founded in 753 BCE, you must add the two numbers together to get 2766 and then add in another one, since 753 BCE was 1 AUC.

Therefore, 2013 is 2767 AUC.

© Prufrock Press Inc. • *Ancient Roots and Ruins*

LESSON 5

CONNECTING TO LITERATURE

Instructional Purpose: To connect the concept of time and monuments to authentic Roman readings.

Horace's poem about the timelessness of great art is itself a testament to the power of words over time. In this lesson, students will examine an authentic piece of Latin literature and analyze the content, theme, and tone of the poem.

ACTIVITIES:

1. Have students read the poem by Horace in Handout 5.1: Horace's Ode.
2. As students read the poem, ask them to underline Latin words they can understand either because of derivatives or from learning the words themselves.
3. Ask students to respond to the poem by answering the following questions:
    a. What Roman religious imagery does Horace use in this poem? Why is that significant in a poem about the ravages of time? If necessary, refer to Chapter 5 for an explanation of terms (e.g., Vestal Virgin, *pontifex maximus*).
    b. Why does he use the muse Melpomene here instead of any other muse? Refer to Chapter 3 to review her identity.
    c. Do you fundamentally think that Horace is right, that written works and ideas outlast physical monuments? Support your answer with examples.

4. Have students list modern monuments (that are not monuments) that you think could be described in a similar way, and will prove to be "more lasting than bronze" (e.g., Shakespeare's sonnets or Munch's painting, *The Scream*). Share and discuss as a whole class.
5. After students have discussed their modern monuments, ask them to compare "*Exegi monumentum*" to "Shall I Compare Thee to a Summer's Day?" in Handout 5.2: Shakespeare's Sonnet in a journal entry about theme, content, and tone.

HANDOUT 5.1

HORACE'S ODE

Quintus Horatius Flaccus (Horace)
Odes, Book III, xxx

Exegi monumentum aere perennius,
regalique situ pyramidum altius,
quod non imber edax, non Aquilo impotens
possit diruere aut innumerabilis
annorum series et fuga temporum.
Non omnis moriar, multaque pars mei
vitabit Libitinam. Usque ego postera
crescam laude recens. Dum Capitolium
scandet cum tacita virgine pontifex.

dicar, qua violens obstrepit Aufidus
et qua pauper aquae daunus agrestium
regnavit populorum ex humili potens,
princeps Aoelium carmen ad Italos
deduxisse modos. Sume superbiam
quaesitam meritis et mihi Delphica
lauro cinge volens, Melpomene, comam.

I have built a monument more lasting than bronze,
And higher than the royal site of the pyramids,
Which neither pelting rains nor the North wind
Can destroy, nor the countless succession of years
And the flight of time.
I will not die entirely and a great part of me will avoid death.
Renewed by praise, I will grow ever in posterity,
As long as the Pontifex Maximus will visit the Capitoline with the silent Vestal
    Virgin.

I will be spoken of, wherever the rushing river Aufidus roars, and wherever pow-
    erful Daunus ruled his people, in days devoid of water.
I, powerful, from humble beginnings, will be thought an emperor for adapting
    Aeolian poetry to Italian meters.
Take the sought after pride, so well-deserved, Melpomene, and willingly crown
    my hair with the wreath of Apollo.

© Prufrock Press Inc. • *Ancient Roots and Ruins*

HANDOUT 5.2

SHAKESPEARE'S SONNET

Sonnet 16
William Shakespeare

Shall I compare thee to a summer's day?
Thou art more lovely and more temperate:
Rough winds do shake the darling buds of May,
And summer's lease hath all too short a date:
Sometime too hot the eye of heaven shines,
And often is his gold complexion dimmed,
And every fair from fair sometime declines,
By chance, or nature's changing course untrimmed:
But thy eternal summer shall not fade,
Nor lose possession of that fair thou ow'st,
Nor shall death brag thou wander'st in his shade,
When in eternal lines to time thou grow'st,
So long as men can breathe, or eyes can see,
So long lives this, and this gives life to thee.

LESSON 6

MYTHOLOGY AND SEASONS

Instructional Purpose: To understand the role of mythology in the Roman concept of seasons.

According to tradition, Romulus, the first king of Rome, measured the year according to moon cycles and seasons. Initially, Romans marked the passing of each season with festivals celebrating specific deities either associated with the time of year, the necessary weather, or the harvest. Later though, these festivals became associated more strongly with specific months and days, and Ovid's *Fasti* tells us much about these.

The Romans, like many other cultures, told stories to explain the seasons. The Roman figures most associated with the changing of the seasons were Proserpina (Persephone in Greek), Pluto (Hades), and Ceres (Demeter). In this lesson, students will explore this myth, as well as the meaning behind it as an explanation of natural phenomena.

ACTIVITIES:

1. Give students access to a modern calendar to answer the following questions.
   a. How do modern calendars show the beginning and end of each season?
   b. Do these revolve around days of special planetary importance (e.g., solstices)?
   c. For the Romans, festivals and school holidays often intersected with these days—do they on our calendar? If so, how?

2. Give students Handout 6.1: The Myth of Springtime and have them answer the following questions.
   a. Is there a moral to this myth? What does it mean? Retitle it to reflect your understanding.
   b. Evaluate the illustration included with the myth—what elements of the story does it convey effectively? What might you add to the illustration to make it clearer?
   c. What does the myth reveal about Greco-Roman values? How could you update the myth to reflect contemporary beliefs?

      d. Why did the Romans need myths? What purpose did they serve?

      e. This myth is largely concerned with two opposing forces, one seemingly on the side of good, the other seemingly on the side of evil, and ends with a compromise. Create a modern myth that explains a natural phenomenon and explores this same concept.

3. Have students share their myths in small groups.

HANDOUT 6.1

THE MYTH OF SPRINGTIME

Ceres, the goddess of the harvest, had a daughter, Proserpina, whom she loved very much. One day, Proserpina wandered with the nymphs, collecting flowers in the fields around Pergusa Lake in Sicily. While she wandered, Pluto, the god of the Underworld, spotted her while coming up from the volcanic Mount Etna on his four-horse chariot. Immediately captured by love of her (probably the fault of Cupid's arrows which cause even gods to fall in love), he flew to her side and flung the maiden over his shoulder, carrying her back to the Underworld to be his queen and sit by his side forever.

Meanwhile, on Earth, Ceres was distraught, searching for her daughter day after day in every corner of the Earth she knew so well. Without a care for anything but her lost child, she stopped tending the harvest. She walked the Earth in search of her Proserpina, ignoring the gods on Mount Olympus and her duty to the grain, fruits, and vegetables that should be growing from the ground. Every step she took in her search became a desert, dried up from her desolation.

Jupiter, the king of the gods, recognized that things could not go on as they were, and sent his son Mercury, the messenger god, to Pluto in the Underworld. Mercury told Pluto of his brother Jupiter's orders, and Pluto, as a subject of his brother's will, had to obey, but not without a plan of his own. Pluto knew that anyone who ate the food of the dead could not return to the world of the living forever. Proserpina had refused food in her depression, but she could not refuse food forever, and Pluto hoped that she would not pass up the innocuous pomegranate seeds left behind on a platter in her chamber. Just as Pluto had hoped, the young woman could not resist the small seeds, and took six, thinking no one would know.

Crafty Pluto struck a deal with Jupiter. He agreed to return her to her mother, but because she had eaten six pomegranate seeds she must come back to him in the Underworld for 6 months out of every year. Ceres was overjoyed to have her daughter back and to know that she was in the world of the living again, no matter the conditions. She began to take care of the Earth again and created the first springtime in her joy at spending time with her daughter. The crops began to grow in the warmth of her love. Buds blossomed, fruit grew, ripening in summer to bring a bountiful harvest as Ceres changed the Earth's colors to Proserpina's favorite—brilliant oranges and reds, knowing her daughter would soon be taken back to the dark and gloomy Underworld. Oranges and reds turn to dull brown as her daughter disappears into the land of the dead, and winter descends as Ceres sinks further into sadness at the loss of her daughter, until the day when she will see her in the springtime and care for the world once again.

© Prufrock Press Inc. • *Ancient Roots and Ruins*

HANDOUT 6.1, CONTINUED

The Romans used this myth to explain the seasonal changes they saw in their world—the change from *ver* (springtime) into *autumnus* (fall) into *hiems* (winter) and *aestas* (summer). Defining seasons according to agriculture and festivals celebrating gods and goddesses became even more important as the Romans divided up their calendar into months, each represented by either a god, a festival, or a number from their system of numerals.

LESSON 7

BIOGRAPHY LESSON

Instructional Purpose: To explore the lives of the Sibyls and oracles and to develop persuasive writing skills.

The Oracles (Greek) and Sibyls (Roman) were women who had the gift of prophecy. The beginning of the line of Sibyls goes back to mythology, but 10 women, associated with different areas of the world, each are depicted in story and art as important oracles who could see through time itself. These women could tell a visitor about his future, as well as realities the visitor needed to face. In this lesson, students will discover the truth behind the story of the Sibyls, as well as their symbolic importance.

ACTIVITIES:

1. Ask students to read the story of the oracles and sibyls and their importance on the King's College website (http://departments. kings.edu/womens_history/ancoracles.html).

2. Next, ask them to read the specific story of Pythia, the first Greek oracle, on Wikipedia (http://en.wikipedia.org/wiki/Pythia), and then read the list of prophecies (http://en.wikipedia.org/wiki/ List_of_oracular_statements_from_Delphi).

3. Ask students to journal on the following prompt: Given the arguments that the oracles and sibyls received their "powers" from gas emissions, develop an argument for why the oracles' words were or were not important in ancient society. You may ask them to consider the power of the self-fulfilling prophecy, as well as the scientific facts surrounding Sibylline inspiration.

4. Michelangelo painted each of the Sibyls in the Sistine Chapel, a famous monument of the Catholic Church. Images of the Sibyls were also incorporated into the ornate stone floor in the Duomo of Siena. Examine the images of these Sibyls online. Divide students into small groups and ask them to explain why they might be an important symbol for other religions, not just Greco-Roman mythology.

5. In these same groups, ask students to read the following quote from Vergil's poetry and research the underlined characters and places before answering the questions below.

> The last age of the Sibyl's song is here.
> The sequence of the ages starts again.
> The past returns—the Virgin, Saturn's realm—
> A new race from High Heaven descends to Earth . . .
> Another <u>Tiphys</u> steers another <u>Argo</u>,
> Laden with heroes; yes, and other wars
> Bring great <u>Achilles</u> once again to <u>Troy</u>.
> (Vergil, Eclogues IV 4–7 and 34–36)

a. What different images does Vergil associate with time in this poem?

b. Why do you think he references Tiphys, the Argo, and Achilles here?

c. Why do you think he references the Sibyl? Why would she be a good poetic representation for time?

LESSON 8

A DAY IN THE LIFE OF A ROMAN

Instructional Purpose: To connect the daily lives of the Romans with the concept of time.

Romans spent their days in varying ways depending on their class, gender, and social or political position. In this lesson, you will examine the different lives that different sectors of society lived and recreate a day in the life of a Roman using Roman hours.

ACTIVITIES:

1. Ask students to research a typical day in the life of a wealthy Roman woman, a wealthy Roman man, a poor Roman man, and a poor Roman woman. They can use the following websites in their research.
   - ThinkQuest (http://library.thinkquest.org/22866/English/Romday/Dagin.html)
   - PBS (http://www.pbs.org/empires/romans/empire/life.html)

   Ask them to discuss as a class what differences there are between the different activities each would participate in during the day. Are there any similarities between any of these four? What does this say about Roman society? Class distinctions?
2. Ask students to journal about the similarities and differences in lifestyle for poor and wealthy Americans vs. Romans, as well as the role of women in society in ancient Rome and modern America.
3. Ask students to create a small, 6-page book of hours, representing any 6 of the 12 hours of Roman daylight. On each page, students should illustrate one hour in the life of each of these four—they may choose which hour to include for each, but captions must use correct Latin to describe the hour of the day (use your work from Lesson 3). The image must show clearly what the member of Roman society is doing at that hour.
4. Ask students to present their books of hours in small groups and justify the importance of their choices.

LESSON 9

TIMES OF LIFE

Instructional Purpose: To compare ancient and modern celebrations of different times of life.

Romans had four basic ceremonies to celebrate different times in a Roman man's life—the naming ceremony, the coming of age ceremony at age 13–14, the wedding ceremony, and the funeral ceremony. In this lesson, students will learn about each ceremony and its connections to the modern world and recreate one in class.

ACTIVITIES:

1. Students should read about each of these four ceremonies at the links below.
   - ThinkQuest (http://library.thinkquest.org/26602/ceremonies.htm)
   - Classics Unveiled (http://www.classicsunveiled.com/romel/html/romechildren.html)

2. Separate students into groups of four to five students. Assign each group one of the stages of life ceremonies. Have each group discuss and reach consensus regarding the answers to the following questions.
   a. What was the significance of this ceremony?
   b. Are there any equivalent ceremonies or similarities between this ceremony and modern celebrations?
   c. What aspects of this ceremony relate to mythology and Roman religion?
   d. What aspects of this ceremony tell us about Roman values?

3. Ask each group of students to create props from either construction paper or found objects necessary to reenact this ceremony, and explain why each prop is important in the ceremony (e.g., for weddings, the knot of Hercules; for funerals, the masks of the ancestors).

4. Next, have each group of students act out the ceremony they are assigned for the whole class. After their reenactment, they must explain their answers to the discussion questions. Grade the presentations using Handout 9.1: Times of Life Project Rubric.

5. Have students individually journal on the following topic: How does recreating and witnessing these celebrations add to your understanding of the Romans and their values?

HANDOUT 9.1

TIMES OF LIFE PROJECT RUBRIC

Category	4	3	2	1
Interactivity and Performance	Successfully uses interactivity to engage most students in the presentation.	Successfully engages some students in the presentation. Incorporates props, etc., but some elements of planned activities may not work well.	Occasionally able to maintain student interest, but unsuccessful with activities overall.	Reads information only. No activities used to aid student understanding.
Quality of Explanation and Discussion Questions	Information clearly relates to the main topic. It addresses all discussion questions and provides supporting evidence.	Information clearly relates to the main topic. Provides some supporting details, but may not include all discussion questions.	Information clearly relates to the main topic. Nearly all questions answered, but no details and/or examples are given.	Responses to questions have little to do with the main topic with no support given.
Visuals (Props, Costumes, Handouts, etc.)	Visuals are given/shown to students and used to great effect in the presentation.	Visuals add to the presentation.	Visual content can distract from the presentation at times.	Visuals are distracting from the presentation topic rather than helpful, or are not included.
			Total	_____ /12

LESSON 10

ROMAN TIMELINES

Instructional Purpose: To synthesize understanding of Roman history and the progression of events over time.

Now that ancient Rome is a part of the past, like Sibyls, we can look through time to examine the natural disasters, characters, and important events that shaped that civilization. Timelines give us a way to sketch out such details and define key elements from the historical record. In this lesson, students will discuss the progression of events in specific periods in Roman history and then create their own visual timeline.

ACTIVITIES:

1. Students should read Chapter 4: History of the Roman Empire. Have students particularly focus on the readings about the Julio-Claudian emperors and look carefully at the timeline in the back of the chapter.
2. Next, students should compare timelines of Roman history, specifically focusing on the 1st century CE using the following websites.
   • Scaruffi (http://www.scaruffi.com/politics/romans.html)
   • Cornell University (http://falcon.arts.cornell.edu/prh3/151/tlinerom.html)
   • Exovedate (http://www.exovedate.com/ancient_timeline_one.html)

3. Students should answer the questions: What are the benefits and drawbacks of the different kinds of timeline? What would your ideal timeline look like?
4. Have students create their own timeline, including the top 10 events of the 1st century CE. They must justify their choice of events, as well as the format of their timeline.
5. Have students debate the most important 10 events of this era and come to a class consensus.
6. Create a collective class timeline, extending around the room if possible. Ask students in pairs or groups to illustrate and label each major event on chart paper. Post in chronological order at the front of the room or around the room.

UNIT ASSESSMENT

1. Give students 45 minutes to write an essay in class on the following topic: Analyze Roman concepts of time and discuss what they reveal about Roman culture. How do modern concepts of time reveal information about modern values? Use specific examples studied in the unit as you craft your response.

2. Ask students to choose one generalization about time from this unit and write about how it applies to their understanding of the Roman concept of time.

RESOURCES

Toynbee, A. (1972). *A study of history*. Oxford, England: Oxford University Press.

http://www.etymonline.com

http://roma.andreapollett.com/S7/roma-cal.htm

http://departments.kings.edu/womens_history/ancoracles.html

http://en.wikipedia.org/wiki/Pythia

http://en.wikipedia.org/wiki/List_of_oracular_statements_from_Delphi

http://library.thinkquest.org/22866/English/Romday/Dagin.html

http://library.thinkquest.org/22866/English/Romday/Dagin.html

http://oldintranet.puhinui.school.nz/Topics/AncientCivs/greecerome/Romeroles1.html

http://www.scaruffi.com/politics/romans.html

http://falcon.arts.cornell.edu/prh3/151/tlinerom.html

http://www.exovedate.com/ancient_timeline_one.html

UNIT 2

SPACE

> *Divide et impera.*
> Divide and conquer.
>
> —Gaius Julius Caesar

CONCEPT OF SPACE

The concept of space in Roman history was often defined by the boundaries of towns and cities, provinces and territories, countries and continents. In other words, space had a strong geographical orientation. The Romans continually conquered other countries, adding to the Roman Empire and using expansion as a synonym for power. Yet at the same time, space was important in defining how Romans lived their daily lives and the areas in which they carried out pleasure and business. A Roman home, for example, was organized to provide space for gathering, for relaxing, and for the daily rituals of eating and sleeping. Public baths were the spaces designated for washing the body and relaxing if you were a Roman male. The forum was a designated city space for commerce in every Roman town. The temple was the designated space for worship.

The Senate House in Rome was the site for governmental work to be carried out. Personal space was also a way of delineating social classes in Rome where women, peons, and slaves had fewer freedoms within the society and thus less space to move in, never being allowed to enter the Senate House or the temple or to attend certain public events.

KEY GENERALIZATIONS

» Space, through physical and human geography, defines the boundaries of Roman power and social structures.
» Spaces within Rome may be perceived as personal, communal, or sacred in Roman society.
» Space may be defined by mapping or physical demarcations.
» Space, defined by Roman conquest, added resources and interaction of ideas that promoted the development of Roman innovation.

ESSENTIAL QUESTIONS

» How did Romans perceive the importance of space, both internally (within Rome) and externally (outside of Rome)?
» How did Romans demarcate conquered spaces and territories?
» How did spatial expansion impact Roman society?
» How do spatial boundaries within a society impact culture?

GOALS AND OUTCOMES

» Develop an appreciation for the role of spatial location and boundaries in Rome's development.

Students will be able to:

• create maps illustrating physical space within Roman houses, the Roman city, and the Roman empire; and
• analyze ancient and modern maps and what they reveal about a culture.

» Develop an understanding of the concept of space.

Students will be able to:
- develop relevant products that apply the Roman concept of space, and
- evaluate ancient beliefs about space.

» Develop critical thinking and reasoning.

Students will be able to:
- evaluate world Roman conquests in relation to other colonial cultures,
- debate the role of geography in determining military outcomes, and
- analyze the impact of different kinds of space.

» Express creative ideas in multiple forms.

Students will be able to:
- create written and visual products that express ideas about space, and
- synthesize multiple forms to create a three-dimensional model of a Roman house.

LESSON 1

SPACE AND EMPIRE

Instructional Purpose: To engage students in discussion of the concept of empire as it relates to space within a culture.

Cultures and countries throughout the ages have tried conquering one another as a way to gain more space of their own, as well as more power. The Romans were no exception, and were more successful than almost any other culture. In Lesson 1, students will explore the concept of space and territory through discussion of authentic Latin writings about conquest.

ACTIVITIES:

1. Ask students to write a journal entry answering the following questions: How would you live if you didn't have personal space (e.g., space between people interacting) or private space (e.g., a room of one's own)? Could you thrive without space? Why or why not? Do you think countries/cultures need a certain amount of space to thrive? Why or why not?

2. Group students into pairs to brainstorm cultures and countries that over time have invaded or conquered other countries. If necessary, prompt them to research the concepts of empire and colonization on the part of the British, French, and Spanish. Then have them research those countries/cultures (or others they identify) and respond to the questions below:
   a. What motivations did these countries have or claim to have in conquering others?
   b. Are there any eras or time periods where more countries are trying to conquer each other, or are they spread out?
   c. Has the conquering culture had an influence on that country over time (e.g., national language, infrastructure, city names, etc.)?

3. The concept of Empire is important in understanding the enduring influence of the Romans in modern culture. Direct students to Handout 1.1: Romani Provinciae Probatio, then (again, in pairs)

ask them to compare the Roman empire to the other empires they discussed in the previous activity. How do the conquered territories compare? Do certain countries seem to have changed hands more than others? If so, why do you think that might be? Are there factors that make certain countries more likely to conquer? Are there factors that make a country more likely to be conquered or sought after?

4. Ask students to share their responses to the last set of questions as a whole group.

5. Next, ask students to read the excerpted passages from Julius Caesar's Book 1 of *De Bello Gallico* (see Handout 1.2) and answer the following questions in small groups.

   a. What reasons does Caesar give in this passage for why some tribes are stronger than others or are more interested in conquering territory than others?

   b. Do you think Caesar is justified in these opinions about what makes a culture strong or weak? Do you fundamentally agree or disagree with him? Why or why not?

   c. What do Caesar's opinions say about Roman values and the way that Romans defined territory?

NAME: _____ **DATE:** _____

HANDOUT 1.1

ROMANI PROVINCIAE PROBATIO

Mihi nomen est _____

Using the map below, fill in the correct Latin name for each of the countries mentioned by number in the Latin questions below. Remember, spelling counts!

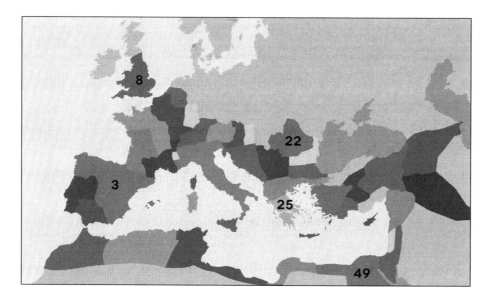

Octo est provincia quam Caesar exploravit primus. Quid est?

_____

Viginti-quinque est provincia quae pugnat cum Roma pro multos annos. Quid est?

_____

Undequinquaginta est colonia antiqua quae Graecae vicit primum. Quid est?

_____

Tres est provincia quae habet maximos populos quae Romanos oppugnant. Quid est?

_____

Viginti-duo est provincia quae habet maximum numerum populi qui Romanos resistant. Quid est?

_____

© Prufrock Press Inc. • _Ancient Roots and Ruins_

NAME: _____   DATE: _____

HANDOUT 1.2

EXCERPT FROM CAESAR'S DE BELLO GALLICO

Gallia est omnis divisa in partes tres, quarum unam incolunt Belgae, aliam Aquitani, tertiam qui ipsorum lingua Celtae, nostra Galli appellantur. Hi omnes lingua, institutis, legibus inter se differunt. Gallos ab Aquitanis Garumna flumen, a Belgis Matrona et Sequana dividit. Horum omnium fortissimi sunt Belgae, propterea quod a cultu atque humanitate provinciae longissime absunt, minimeque ad eos mercatores saepe commeant atque ea quae ad effeminandos animos pertinent important, proximique sunt Germanis, qui trans Rhenum incolunt, quibuscum continenter bellum gerunt. Qua de causa Helvetii quoque reliquos Gallos virtute praecedunt, quod fere cotidianis proeliis cum Germanis contendunt, cum aut suis finibus eos prohibent aut ipsi in eorum finibus bellum gerunt.

All Gaul is divided into three parts, one of which the Belgae inhabit, the Aquitani another, those who in their own language are called Celts, in our Gauls, the third. All these differ from each other in language, customs, and laws. The river Garonne separates the Gauls from the Aquitani; the Marne and the Seine separate them from the Belgae. Of all these, the Belgae are the bravest, because they are furthest from the civilization and refinement of [our] Province, and merchants least frequently resort to them, and import those things which tend to effeminate the mind; and they are the nearest to the Germans, who dwell beyond the Rhine, with whom they are continually waging war; for which reason the Helvetii also surpass the rest of the Gauls in valor, as they contend with the Germans in almost daily battles, when they either repel them from their own territories, or themselves wage war on their frontiers.

Caesar's *De Bello Gallico*, Book I, Chapter One
Translation by W. A. McDevitte and W. S. Bohn
Retrieved from http://classics.mit.edu/Caesar/gallic.1.1.html

LESSON 2

MAPS

Instructional Purpose: To allow students to explore maps from a variety of perspectives, as creators and evaluators.

Ancient and modern maps can tell us much about the land pictured, but they also reveal information about the author of the map, or cartographer. In this lesson, students will compare maps of the modern and ancient world as well as create their own.

ACTIVITIES:

1. Ask each student to use chart paper to sketch out a map that illustrates the space between their home and school. Ask them to mark out any street names, important landmarks or geographical features between the two locations. Do not allow more than 15 minutes for sketching.

2. Put students into pairs in which each presents their map to the other. Have partners answer the following questions after seeing the presenter's map.
    a. How do the two maps differ, both geographically and in terms of landmarks, features, etc. provided?
    b. What clues are there to the identity of your partner within the map? Are there landmarks or features that say something about what is or is not important to them?
    c. Could you pick this map out of a line-up as reflecting your partner in some way?

3. Pick a few students to share out their partner's maps, particularly noting how differences in values are illustrated within the map (e.g., McDonald's noted as a landmark versus a parent's workplace).

4. Now have students refer to the University of Texas website (http://www.lib.utexas.edu/maps/index.html) for authentic images of Roman maps. Then have students answer the following questions in small groups and share their responses.

    a. Are there similarities between Roman names for continents and modern names for continents? What about countries?

    b. What can you tell about the mapmaker's values or Roman values by looking at these examples?

5. Now, go back to the timeline you created in the previous unit. Choose an ancient map from the website that covers the area around the Mediterranean Sea. Mark on the map important sites mentioned in your timeline of the history of Rome, particularly noting sites of conquest for the Romans.

6. In small groups, share examples of the maps you have worked on. Respond to the following questions in your group.

    a. Is there a pattern to Roman conquests as discerned by the maps analyzed?

    b. What generalizations can you make about Roman expansion, given the map changes across the years?

LESSON 3

LATIN VOCABULARY AND USAGE

Instructional Purpose: To practice the language of the Romans concerning geography and the vocabulary of conquered territories.

The ancient Romans used specific words to describe the lands that they conquered, both by naming them in the Roman way and by designating what special benefits and infrastructure they could receive from Rome. A conquered territory could be deemed a *municipium* (local town or territory), *provincia* (province), or a *colonia* (colony). In this lesson, students will map out the modern vocabulary of conquest, as well as its ancient roots.

ACTIVITIES:

1. Ask students to complete a copy of Handout 3.1: Vocabulary Web for each of the following words.
   - conquest
   - civilization
   - culture
   - society
   - location

   For the following, students must give a deeper root than the Latin words listed above, using Wiktionary (http://www.wiktionary.org) as their source for roots and stems (e.g., procrastination comes from three Latin words strung together—*pro*, meaning "for," *cras*, meaning "tomorrow," and *teneo*, meaning "hold," therefore meaning "to hold off for tomorrow").
   - province
   - colony
   - municipality

2. Ask students to read Handout 3.2: Roman Names for Countries.
3. Ask students to use their knowledge of geography (and perhaps extra maps) to try to answer the questions at the bottom of Handout 1.1: Romani Provinciae Probatio in Latin.

4. In preparation for activities in both Unit 2 and Unit 3, students must select a Roman territory that they will feel comfortable researching for an extended period.

5. Now, give students Handout 3.3: Latin Phrases. Ask the students to identify why all of the adjective forms of places have endings of us/a/um on the end of them. Remind them that every noun in Latin, and every person has a gender, so boys (*pueri*) must have a masculine ending to describe their citizenship (*Aegyptianus*) while girls (*puellae*) must have a feminine ending (*Aegyptiana*).

6. Ask students to use the pronunciation guide in Appendix A to practice saying the citizenship they have claimed.

7. Refer students to the bottom of Handout 3.3: Latin Phrases and have them practice saying these phrases appropriately: *ego sum, tu es, illa est,* and *ille est.*

8. Next, have them attach the correct form of the adjective describing their fictional citizenship (e.g., *ego sum Aegyptiana* if student is a girl or *ego sum Aegyptianus* if student is a boy).

9. Have each student create a table-tent for themselves with their phrase in Latin. These will be used again in Unit 3.

HANDOUT 3.1

VOCABULARY WEB

Vocabulary Web

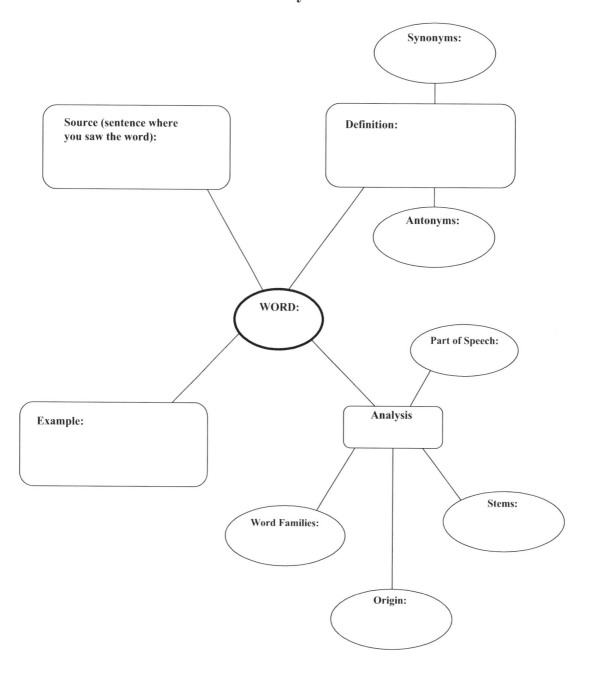

Center for Gifted Education
The College of William and Mary

© Prufrock Press Inc. • *Ancient Roots and Ruins*

HANDOUT 3.2

ROMAN NAMES FOR COUNTRIES

Egypt	Aegyptus
England	Britannia
France	Gallia
Germany	Germania
Greece	Graeca
Ireland	Hibernia
Israel	Judaea
Northern Africa	Libya
Portugal	Lusitania
Romania	Dacia
Scotland	Caledonia
Spain	Hispania
Turkey	Anatolia

HANDOUT 3.3

LATIN PHRASES

Ego sum (I am). . .
Tu es (you are). . .
illa (she)/ille (he) est (is). . .

Aegyptianus/Aegyptiana
Britannicus/Britannica
Gallicus/Gallica
Germanicus/Germanica
Graecus/Graeca
Hibernianus/Hiberniana
Judaicus/Judaica
Libyanus/Libyana
Lusitanicus/Lusitanica
Dacianus/Daciana
Caledonianus/Caledoniana
Hispanicus/Hispanica
Anatolianus/Anatoliana

© Prufrock Press Inc. • *Ancient Roots and Ruins*

LESSON 4

BIOGRAPHY STUDY: HANNIBAL AND CLEOPATRA

Instructional Purpose: To study the lives of famous conquerors whom Rome defeated.

In this lesson, students will read about Hannibal and Cleopatra, two famous people from geographical territories the Romans conquered.

ACTIVITIES:

1. Have students complete Handout 4.1: Biography Chart for Hannibal and Cleopatra, consulting the following websites.
   - Wikipedia (en.wikipedia.org/wiki)
   - Encyclopedia Brittanica (http://www.britannica.com)
   - Open Library (http://www.openlibrary.org)

2. Ask the groups to report on key aspects of each life.
3. Ask students the following discussion questions.
   a. What aspects of the background of Hannibal and Cleopatra indicated what role they might assume in their societies?
   b. How did they each prepare for the roles that they assumed in society?
   c. What original contributions did each make?
   d. How important was geography in contributing to the rise and fall of these two great leaders? Explain.
   e. What have we learned from these biographies about the concept of space?

4. Have students write a 10-minute journal entry on the role of geopolitics in our society. Share some examples and discuss.

5. Now ask students to complete the comparative analysis chart below on Hannibal and Cleopatra in small groups.

	Hannibal	Cleopatra
Qualities of leadership		
Vision		
Use of symbols		
Relationships with people		
Effectiveness in war and peace		

6. Based on the chart, have the groups construct an argument that suggests that one or the other is the better leader of Carthage or Egypt. Ask student groups to share their perspectives.

HANDOUT 4.1

BIOGRAPHY CHART

Name of person:_____

Birth date and death date:_____

Family members (at birth):_____

Extended family (e.g., spouse, children):_____

_____

Early education/continued education:_____

Interests and predispositions:_____

_____

Personality characteristics:_____

_____

Abilities: _____

_____

Role he or she played in Roman history:_____

_____

_____

Contributions:_____

Important quotes (3–5):_____

_____

_____

Awards and honors:_____

Why is he or she still remembered today?_____

_____

_____

LESSON 5

ROMAN ROADS

Instructional Purpose: To engage students directly in their own research on the topic of Roman roads and the materials used to build them through the use of a problem-based learning (PBL) episode.

Romans were certainly not the first to build roads to connect the spaces they conquered, nor were they the first to establish roads in their home territories. However, they used new methods as they began the process of building roads, and Roman roads became so well known that the phrase "*Omnes viae Romam ducunt*" or "All roads lead to Rome" is used to this day. In this lesson, students will engage in a problem-based learning scenario, researching the engineering of Roman roads.

Note: The activities described below require the use of PBL as a model. If you are unfamiliar with PBL, please see Handout 5.1: Problem-Based Learning for more information on what it entails and how it works.

ACTIVITIES:

1. Give students the following PBL prompt.

    > Problem: You are a Celtic engineer that works with the Romans in Britannia. The proconsul of Britannia has just asked you to design and oversee the construction of a road from *Londinium* (London) to *Camalodunum* (Colchester). Your superior thinks you should use Roman methods and materials because it is for the Romans and that you should use the Appian Way in Rome as your model, but your tribe leader wants you to use local materials. A new temple is about to be built 20 miles out from *Londinium* and must be included on the route of the road, but negotiations with the builders are stalled. You have 2 days to develop a design to present to the proconsul. What do you do?

2. Students should work through Handout 5.2: Need to Know Board in small groups for items they must research.

3. Ask them to report their plan of action on charts. Comment and critique as a class.

4. Have students work through a secondary plan to answer the questions raised by assigning info searches to group members, deciding on the format for the project report components and the nature of the model they are going to build.

5. Provide secondary resources for the groups to read and online websites that will assist them in their work.
   - HistoryToday (http://www.historytoday.com/logan-thompson/roman-roads)
   - Roman Sites (http://www.romansites.com/)
   - Crystalinks (http://www.crystalinks.com/romeroads.html)
   - Britain Express (http://www.britainexpress.com/History/Roman_Roads.htm)

6. Provide a deadline for the work, based on the scenario and how much time you feel the project should last, given the tasks. Recommended time frame: 2 weeks.

7. Ask students to complete Handout 5.3: Problem Log Questions individually as a journaling exercise after they have done the first day of research.

8. Have a day when students share in groups their resolution to the problem. Display their models of the road and any maps they have created in the room or in the school.

9. Ask all students to reflect on the questions in Handout 5.4: Questions for Reflection.

HANDOUT 5.1

PROBLEM-BASED LEARNING

Problem-based learning is a curriculum and instructional model that is highly constructivist in design and execution. First used in the medical profession to better socialize doctors to patient's real-world concerns, it is now selectively employed in educational settings at elementary and secondary levels with gifted learners (Boyce, VanTassel-Baska, Burruss, Sher, & Johnson, 1997; Gallagher & Stepien, 1996; Gallagher, 1998). The technique involves several important features:

- Students are in charge of their own learning. By working in small investigatory teams, they grapple with a real-world unstructured problem that they have a stake in and must solve within a short period of time. Students become motivated to learn because they are in charge at every stage of the process.

- The problem statement is ambiguous, incomplete, and yet appealing to students because of its real-world quality and the stakeholder role that they assume in it. For example, students may be given roles as scientists, engineers, politicians, or important project-based administrators whose job it is to deal with the problem expeditiously.

- The role of the teacher is facilitative rather than directive, aiding students primarily through asking questions and providing additional scaffolding of the problem with new information or resources needed. The teacher becomes a metacognitive coach, urging students through probing questions to deepen their inquiry.

- The students complete Handout 5.2: Need to Know Board early in their investigation, allowing them to plan out how they will attack the problem, first by identifying what they already know from the problem statement, what they need to know, and how they will find it out. They then can prioritize what they need to know, make assignments, and set up timelines for the next phase of work. Such an emphasis on constructed metacognitive behavior is central to the learning benefits of the approach.

These features work together in engaging the learner in important problems that matter in their world. Many times, problems are constructed around specific situations involving pollution of water or air, dangerous chemicals, spread of infectious disease, or energy source problems. Students learn that the real world requires an interdisciplinary orientation, demanding the use of many different thinking skills and many different kinds of expertise in order to solve problems.

© Prufrock Press Inc. • *Ancient Roots and Ruins*

HANDOUT 5.1, CONTINUED

In order to work through a problem-based learning episode, students must be able to analyze, synthesize, evaluate, and create—all higher level thinking tasks according to Anderson, Krathwohl & Bloom (2000). The following problem and its levels of complex thinking are illustrative of a problem-based learning episode.

> Problem: You are a Celtic engineer that works with the Romans in Britannia. The proconsul of Britannia has just asked you to design and oversee the construction of a road from *Londinium* (London) to *Camalodunum* (Colchester). Your superior thinks you should use Roman methods and materials because it is for the Romans, but your tribe leader wants you to use local materials. A new temple is about to be built 20 miles out from *Londinium* and must be included on the route of the road, but negotiations with the builders are stalled. You have two days to develop a design to present to the proconsul. What do you do?

Higher level skills needed to address the problem include:

- analysis of what the real problem is: local politics, road construction, materials?
- synthesis of the aspects of the problem—is there a creative synthesis of each facet of the problems noted?
- evaluation of alternative strategies to be employed—can I shift funds, can I employ a transportation expert, can I deal with the temple? and
- creation of the plan of action that will need to be sold to the proconsul.

REFERENCES

Boyce, L. N., VanTassel-Baska, J., Burrus, J. D., Sher, B. T., & Johnson, D. T. (1997). A problem-based curriculum: Parallel learning opportunities for students and teachers. *Journal for the Education of the Gifted, 20*, 363–379.

Gallagher, J. J. (1998). Preparing the gifted students as independent learners. In J. Leroux (Ed.), *Connecting with the gifted community: Selected proceedings from the 12th World Conference of the World Council for Gifted and Talented Children, Inc.* Ottawa, Canada: Faculty of Education, University of Ottawa.

Gallagher, S. A., & Stepien, W. J. (1996). Content acquisition in problem-based learning: Depth versus breadth in American Studies. *Journal for the Education of the Gifted, 19*(3), 257-275.

HANDOUT 5.2

NEED TO KNOW BOARD

What do you know?	What do you need to know?	How are you going to find out?

© Prufrock Press Inc. • *Ancient Roots and Ruins*

HANDOUT 5.3
PROBLEM LOG QUESTIONS

What have you learned about Roman road building that you will apply to your problem?

_____

_____

_____

_____

_____

What have you learned about the terrain or materials of Britain that affects your decision making?

_____

_____

_____

_____

_____

What are the next steps for dealing with your problem?

_____

_____

_____

_____

_____

_____

HANDOUT 5.4

QUESTIONS FOR REFLECTION

What have you learned from this PBL episode? Please comment on content learning and what it taught you as a learner.

_____

_____

_____

_____

_____

_____

What did you learn about working in groups from this project?

_____

_____

_____

_____

_____

_____

How can you improve your project-based work in the future, based on this experience?

_____

_____

_____

_____

_____

_____

© Prufrock Press Inc. • *Ancient Roots and Ruins*

LESSON 6

VOCABULARY OF HOME SPACE

Instructional Purpose: To help students understand private spaces in the ancient world and create their own replica.

Romans in different levels of society lived very differently from one another, both in terms of the space they had in their dwelling and how that space was used. Poor people lived in an *insula*, or apartment building (interestingly, *insula* is also the word for island in Latin). These usually were designed to have one large room that could be used as a bedroom/dining room/living room and a kitchen. Middle-class Romans lived in a *domus* (house), which usually featured individual rooms for the bedroom, dining room, living room, and kitchen. A wealthy Roman, however, would have an extravagant country estate, called a villa, which contained various rooms for various purposes. In this lesson, students will research the rooms of a Roman house and create a blueprint for an authentic Roman villa, using measurements to scale.

ACTIVITIES:

1. Have students research the rooms and decorations of a Roman villa at the following websites.
   * Virtual Visit to Torre Llauder (http://www.viaavgvsta.anonai.com/VVTLL1en.html)
   * Roman Britain (http://www.romanbritain.freeserve.co.uk/villa.htm)

2. Students should compare the rooms and elements of the Roman villa with the rooms and elements of their own houses. Are their major similarities? Differences? What do these say about each society?
3. Have each student create a blueprint for his or her own Roman villa, using graph paper, which incorporates all of the rooms and elements from Handout 6.1: Villa Romana Project. Label each room and object carefully.
4. If students have time and resources, ask them to use found objects and materials such as construction paper or cardboard to

create their own Roman villa. Refer to Handout 6.1: Villa Romana Project for explicit instructions.

5. After completing the project, ask students to reflect on the following questions.

    a. What did you learn about the Romans from creating your own Roman-style home?

    b. What spaces within the villa do you think a Roman would use for work? For religion? For food? For entertaining guests?

    c. What do these spaces tell you about Roman values?

HANDOUT 6.1

VILLA ROMANA PROJECT

For this project, you will be building your own Roman villa in miniature. Each Roman villa must include the basic rooms/items mentioned below, and all rooms/items must be properly labeled in Latin and spelled correctly.

Atrium: entrance hall
Compluvium: skylight in the atrium for water to fall into the impluvium
Impluvium: fountain water falls into
Triclinium: dining room
Peristylium: courtyard
Lararium: shrine to the household gods
Culina: kitchen
Cubiculum: singular/Cubicula—bedroom/bedrooms
Tablinum: study

1. Create a blueprint for your villa, drawn and designed in a way that will be easy to copy, with all items and rooms drawn and labeled. (10 pts)
2. Create a list of materials you plan to use to create your villa in 3D and revise your villa blueprint (if necessary). (5 pts)
3. Create your own villa from found objects and/or construction paper and cardboard, which includes all of the items/rooms from your blueprint. Your villa will be graded on the following.

Blueprint drawn and labeled	10 pts
List of materials for 3D villa	5 pts
Accuracy of spelling and labeling	10 pts
Accuracy of room function	10 pts
Items included in rooms (not just four walls)	10 pts
Size of project (small-scale, but all elements visible)	5 pts
Total:	50 pts

LESSON 7

MYTHOLOGY

Instructional Purpose: To explore the mythology of creation and natural space and develop an understanding of Roman values.

The myth of creation in any culture usually discusses the spaces we know in the modern world and where they came from—how the land, sea and sky came to be, who came to rule it and how. In Creation myths, we see how space was defined by a culture in the most basic sense. In this lesson, students will examine myths of creation and territory, as well as how they affected the Roman worldview.

ACTIVITIES:

1. Ask students to research the story of Chaos and Gaea, the origin story of Greco-Roman mythology.

2. Have students to create an illustration that could be included with the myth—one that illustrates the characters, the setting, and the central ideas of the origin story.

3. After completing the illustrations, pair students up and ask them to justify their choices for how they depicted the characters, theme, and the setting for the story. What elements of the story did they convey and how? What details could be added to the illustration to make it clearer?

4. In these same pairs, ask students to respond to the following prompts.
   a. What does the myth reveal about Greco-Roman values?
   b. How could you update the myth to reflect contemporary beliefs/knowledge? Ask students to write a journal entry in response to this question. Share a few responses and discuss as a whole class.

5. Ask students to review the story of how Jupiter, Neptune, and Pluto drew lots for their various domains of the sky, the sea, and the Underworld. Then ask the students to respond to the following prompts in small groups. After discussion, ask a few to share responses from their tables.

a. Was drawing lots an ultimately fair way to decide on each domain?

b. Do you think each domain has equal value? Why or why not? Justify your decision.

c. Do you think it is significant that none of the gods are given dominion over land?

d. What does this story suggest about how Romans viewed space?

LESSON 8

ASTROLOGY

Instructional Purpose: To connect Roman mythology with scientific names for planets and constellations and the practices of astrology and astronomy.

Each of the planets in the solar system (Mercury, Venus, Earth, Mars, Jupiter, Saturn, Uranus, Neptune), with the notable exception of Earth, is named for a Roman god, due to special characteristics of each planet. For example, Mercury is the fastest-moving planet, so ancient stargazers named it for the messenger god, who was depicted with winged sandals. Venus, one of the brightest objects in the night sky, was associated with the goddess of love and beauty. Mars has a dark red tone that is associated with blood, so it was named after the god of war. Jupiter, as the biggest planet by far, was named after the king of the gods. When they discovered the planet Saturn (whose namesake is associated with the Greek Cronus), they decided to name it after the father of Jupiter. Uranus, discovered centuries later by European astronomers, was named for the original god of the sky (associated with the color blue), who was also the father of Saturn. When naming the planets in order, they decided when they found Uranus to keep the genealogy going and name the planet to the right after the father of the planet to the left (Jupiter, son of Saturn, son of Cronus). However, when they discovered Neptune, they realized that they needed another god associated with blue, so it was named after the god of the sea.

Just as each planet and most of their moons are named for mythological beings, so too are the constellations of stars in the sky, some of which make up the zodiac. The zodiac refers to the path of the sun over the course of a year, and the zodiac symbols in many cultures each represent a different week or month in the calendar.

ACTIVITIES:

1. Put students into groups of six and ask each group to take two of the astrological signs and research the mythology or symbolism behind the astrological sign and the actual shape of the sign in the

sky. (Students may choose to use iPad or iPhone/Android apps, if available for this purpose; e.g., NightSky.)

2. Using markers, students should create a drawing on chart paper of the constellation, without marking out the shape that the ancient Greeks and Romans saw.

3. In pencil, students should trace the traditional shape for the astrological sign, then answer the following questions in their groups:

    a. Would you see the same image in this constellation? Why or why not?

    b. Why might another culture have seen this differently? Are there scientific and cultural reasons for this?

    c. Given the shift over time, what images do you think should replace these two zodiacs of ancient imagery and mythology?

4. Each group should share its charts and information about each constellation.

5. In groups, students should create their own proposal for a new zodiac form. The proposal should include information about why their new system of 12 signs is necessary, how it relates to the original Roman zodiac, and why it is important and relevant to a modern audience. Their proposed zodiac can be based on animals, modern heroes, important events, etc.

6. Ask students to share their proposals in group presentations.

LESSON 9

THE ANCIENT FORM OF DEBATE

Instructional Purpose: To develop argument in oral form and understand the connection of issues in Roman society to our own.

ACTIVITIES:

1. Ask students to form debate teams of four and prepare their debate, one period in class and one out of class. Ask each member of the team to prepare according to the following model:
   - 1st affirmative (5 minutes)
   - 1st negative (rebuttal; 3 minutes)
   - 2nd affirmative (3 minutes)
   - Recap of overall argument (5 minutes)

2. Debate the topic of taxation in class teams, using this formal debate style. The proposition is as important now as it was in ancient Rome.

Proposition: Should Rome have expanded its territory beyond its original boundaries? Consider both the effect on local territories, languages and cultures as well as the larger world culture.

PEER AND TEACHER ASSESSMENT:

Ask students to assess each debate presented according to the following criteria.

Soundness of the arguments	3	2	1
Organization of the evidence	3	2	1
Effectiveness of the delivery	3	2	1
Quality of the evidence used	3	2	1
Strengths			
Weaknesses			

Teachers will use the same form to provide feedback to the debate teams on their performance.

LESSON 10

THE ROLE OF CITIES IN ESTABLISHING CIVILIZATIONS

Instructional Purpose: To help students understand the role of Rome's institutions in promoting the growth and development of the Roman Empire.

According to the historian Arnold Toynbee, great civilizations evolve outward from great cities. Thus, in order to understand the triumphs of the Roman civilization, one must understand the strength of the institutions that were established in Rome and replicated throughout the provinces. A capital city of a universal state serves as a melting pot for alien cultures and religions, whose peoples are attracted to it by the facilities it offers, which include the diversity of its population and its role as the center of communication for diffusion of culture. It is through this function that Rome found its lasting link with the future and its historic significance.

ACTIVITIES:

1. Have students consider the list of institutions that were established in Rome and research how they were replicated in France, Britain, and Spain (see Handout 10.1: Roman Institutions). In order to complete the chart in pairs, students should work to explore the following sites: *Lugdunum* (Lyon) and *Arausio* (Orange) in France, *Barca* (Barcelona) and *Caesaraugusta* (Zaragoza) in Spain, *Londinium* (London) and *Camalodunum* (Colchester) in Britain.
2. After completing the chart, ask students to write a reflective journal entry that considers how these provincial areas still retain Roman remains and artifacts that speak to their direct influence on the country as a whole.
3. Have students discuss in small groups the following questions.
   a. Based on your research, what of Roman institutions still remains in the countries of France, Spain, and Britain?

b. In what ways do these remains speak to the early history of these societies? Not all cities exert the degree of influence that Rome did on its neighbors. Consider the factors that put Rome in a leadership position in the ancient world.

c. If Toynbee is right, that communication of ideas is central to a civilization's influence, consider the different ways that ideas were communicated in ancient Rome. How many ways were there that you have learned about so far, and why have some ideas lasted when others haven't?

HANDOUT 10.1

ROMAN INSTITUTIONS

Architectural Engineering Arena, nearby aqueduct "Pont du Gard," Roman theatre, baths	
Roman Law/Government Proconsulships, used as headquarters for Roman emperors during military campaigns	
Roman Art Mosaics in villas, Statues in forum, decorative use of classical columns	
Roman Community Structures Villas, Forum (marketplace), Insula, Domus, Tabernae (shops)	
Roman Religion Temples to Jupiter	
Roman Language Inscriptions on funeral monuments	

© Prufrock Press Inc. • *Ancient Roots and Ruins*

UNIT ASSESSMENT

1. Give students 45 minutes to write an essay in class on the following topic: Analyze the Roman concept of space and discuss what it reveals about Roman culture. How do modern concepts of space reveal information about modern values? Use specific examples studied in the unit as you craft your response.

2. Ask students to choose one generalization about space from this unit and write about how it applies to their understanding of the Roman concept of space (allow 30 minutes for the assessment activity).

RESOURCES

http://www.en.wikipedia.org/wiki

http://www.britannica.com

http://www.Openlibrary.org

http://www.viaavgvsta.anonai.com/VVTLL1en.html

http://www.romanbritain.freeserve.co.uk/villa.htm

http://www.historytoday.com/logan-thompson/roman-roads

http://www.romansites.com/

http://www.crystalinks.com/romeroads.html

http://www.britainexpress.com/History/Roman_Roads.htm

http://www.wiktionary.org

UNIT 3

POWER

Nemo autem regere potest nisi qui et regi.
No one can rule without also being ruled.

—Seneca

CONCEPT OF POWER

The Romans are largely remembered as a power-hungry culture, full of megalomaniacal rulers (kings, dictators, consuls, and emperors) all looking to conquer as much of the world as possible. Although conquest is one aspect of power, there are many other facets to our understanding of power in the ancient world. In this unit, students will consider the power structures inherent in Roman families and Roman society at large. Additionally, students will examine the stories of power, both historical and mythological, and how power is communicated, through both language and the visual arts.

145

KEY GENERALIZATIONS

» Power defined the hierarchy of Roman society.
» Power and the quest for it fueled Roman ambition to conquer other domains.
» Power provided the access to personal freedoms within Roman society.
» Power may be derived from persuasion, family background, role designation, and military or economic position.

ESSENTIAL QUESTIONS

» How did Romans perceive the importance of various kinds of power—political, economic, personal, and persuasive?
» How did Romans define power structures?
» Why is power an important concept in understanding the importance of the Romans?
» How did Roman power structures positively and negatively affect the Roman state?

GOALS AND OUTCOMES

» Develop an understanding of power structures within Roman society.

Students will be able to:
• analyze visual and literary artifacts illustrating Roman power structures, and
• evaluate ancient and modern political structures and what they reveal about power in a culture.

» Develop an understanding of the concept of power in Roman civilization.

Students will be able to:
• develop relevant products that apply the Roman concept of power, and
• evaluate ancient beliefs about power and associated concepts.

» Develop critical thinking and reasoning.

Students will be able to:

- compare Roman social power structures to contemporary U.S. models,
- debate the necessity of supreme political powers on the world stage, and
- analyze the ways in which Roman cultural ideas gained power over time.

» Express creative ideas in multiple forms.

Students will be able to:

- create written and visual products that demonstrate key concepts, and
- synthesize multiple forms to create propaganda for Roman power.

LESSON 1

CONCEPT LESSON

Instructional Purpose: To explore the connection between power and language.

Power can be derived from many sources. The Romans acquired power through various means, conquering territory, learning from other civilizations, and building strength within the city of Rome. In this activity, students will discuss the meaning of power and how it is used.

ACTIVITIES:

1. Ask students to analyze the quotation "Knowledge itself is power" in small groups. As they do, have them consider the following sets of questions.
   a. In your experience, is this quotation correct? Can you name situations in which this quotation was proven correct or incorrect?
   b. Are certain kinds of knowledge more powerful, or more valued, than others?
   c. What makes certain people more powerful or effective than others?
   d. Are there other abstract concepts that you think are more important to power than knowledge (e.g., money, politics, family)?

2. Have students share responses from their small-group discussion as a whole class. List abstract concepts students name as related to power on chart paper at the front of the class.

3. Next, have students number the list in order of importance individually. Then ask them to share their ordered lists and justify their decisions within their small groups.

4. Ask students to read the chapter on language at the beginning of the book, then write a free-response journal entry for 15–20 minutes using this prompt: The Latin quotation "*ipsa scientia potestas est*" (knowledge itself is power) comes not from a Roman, but from an English philosopher and scientist who chose to write

in Latin, as it was the language of intellectual power at the time. What role does language play in power? What makes some languages more powerful than others?

LESSON 2

GRAMMAR/USAGE LESSON

Instructional Purpose: To put into practice language structures necessary for discussing power or the lack of it in ancient Rome.

One way that Romans showed their power was by conquering other territories and capturing slaves from those territories, either to serve them in their homes and businesses or teach their children. In the next lesson, students will each take on the persona of a slave from the ancient Roman world, specifically from the provinces they chose in the "Space" unit. To prepare for this, review language structures from the "Space" and "Time" units to ensure that students can introduce themselves in terms of their ages, backgrounds, heritage, and special skills.

ACTIVITIES:

1. Ask students to take out the table-tents they created in Unit 2, Lesson 3, and refer to Handout 3.1: Vocabulary Web and Handout 3.2: Roman Names for Countries from that lesson to review and practice stating their nationality again (e.g., "*Sum Aegyptianus,*" "*Sum Graeca,*" etc.).

2. Write the following phrases on the board at the front of the room and have students practice repeating them:
   Mihi nomen est_____
   (My name is)
   Mihi lingua est_____
   (My language is)
   Annos natos mihi sunt_____
   (I am . . . years old)

3. Students should decide what age their persona would be and a Roman name to adopt for themselves (consult Handout 2.1: Latina Nomina). Some students may want to choose other names, but remember that a Roman slave from another country would be given a Roman name. Numbers should be given in Roman numerals, as well as Latin, so that they can speak their age in Latin and also write it in Roman numerals. Languages should use the

feminine forms used in the Space unit to agree with the gender of the word *lingua* (e.g., *"Mihi lingua est Britannica," "Mihi lingua est Aegyptiana"*).

4. Next, have students memorize all three phrases so that they will be able to fluently use them in the Roman Daily Life activity in Lesson 3.

5. Have students examine the word *mihi* in both phrases. What does it seem to mean in both? Give students the literal translation for *mihi* as "to me" or "unto me." What do they now think the literal translation for the two sentences would be?

   Key: The name/language unto me is _____. There are unto me _____ birth years.

6. Ask students to reflect on the language structures in these two phrases by discussing the following questions as a class.
   a. What can you infer about Latin word order from these two?
   b. Does it change what part of a sentence is emphasized the most in Latin?
   c. If so, how are certain words given more power?

7. Now students should prepare the persona they chose for the slave market by taking the information they created in Lesson 2 and beginning to fill out Handout 2.2: Titulus on paper. If there is time, students may construct these out of cardboard and string that they can wear around their neck for the following day.

8. Students should review Handout 2.3: Possible Professions in Slavery, choose a profession for their persona, and begin to think about what a typical day in the life of that kind of slave might look like, writing down a possible activity for each hour of the waking day.

9. Ask students to share their list of daily activities, compare them with other students' activities, and use these to discuss their assumptions about Roman slavery.

HANDOUT 2.1

LATINA NOMINA

Adamus: Adam
Adria: Audrey
Adrianus: Adrian
Aemilia: Emily
Aeneas: Angus
Alannus: Alan
Alicia: Alice
Alianora: Eleanor
Alitia: Alice
Aloysius: Lewis
Amabilia: Mabel
Ambrosius: Ambrose
Amia: Amy
Andreas: Andrew
Anna: Ann
Antonius: Anthony
Arcturus: Arthur
Barnabas: Barnabas
Barnabus: Barnaby
Bartolomaeus: Bartholomew
Beatrix: Betteris
Benedictus: Bennet
Benedictus: Benedict
Beniaminus: Benjamin
Brigitta: Bridget
Caecilia: Cecily
Caelia: Celia
Caritas: Charity
Carolus: Carol
Catalina: Catherine
Catherina: Katherine
Caecilia: Cecily
Christiana: Christian
Christopherus: Christopher
Clemens: Clement
Clementia: Clemency
Coelia: Celia
Constantia: Constance
Constans: Constant

Constantius: Constant
Cornelius: Cornelius
Davidus: David
Davus: David
Diana: Diana
Dionysia: Denise
Dionysius: Dennis
Dorothea: Dorothy
Elena: Ellen
Eleanora: Eleanor
Ethelreda: Audrey
Eustacius: Eustace
Felicia: Phillis
Felix: Felix
Ferdinandus: Ferdinando
Fida: Faith
Florens: Florence
Franciscus: Francis
Francisca: Frances
Fridericus: Frederick
Galfridus: Geoffrey
Gaufridus: Geoffrey
Gratia: Grace
Griselda: Grizzel
Hadrianus: Adrian
Hannoria: Hannah
Helena: Helen
Honoria: Honor
Katalina: Katherine
Katharina: Katherine
Laura: Lore
Laurentius: Lawrence
Lucia: Lucy
Marcus: Mark
Maria: Mary
Marianna: Mary Ann
Marina: Marina
Martinus: Martin
Matilda: Maud

© Prufrock Press Inc. • *Ancient Roots and Ruins*

Mauritius: Maurice
Octavius: Octavius
Patentia: Patience
Petronella: Parnel
Petrus: Peter
Phillida: Phillis
Phillipus: Philip
Phineas: Phineas
Placentia: Pleasant
*Ricardus :*Richard
Ricus: Rhys
Rosa: Rose
Rosamunda: Rosamund

Scientia: Sense
Septimus: Septimus
Sextus: Sextus
Sibylla: Sibyl
Spes: Hope
Stephanus: Stephen
Sylvanus: Sylvanus
Terentius: Terrence
Thomasina: Tamsin
Timotheus: Timothy
Tobias: Toby
Ursula: Ursula

HANDOUT 2.2

TITULUS

Mihi nomen est _____ .

_____ *annos natos mihi sunt.*

Sum _____

Lingua mihi est _____ .

Mihi opus est _____ .

Example:
Mihi nomen est Davus. (My name is Davus.)
XX annos natos mihi sunt. (I am 20 years old.)
Sum Britannicus. (I am from the province of Britannia.)
Lingua mihi est Britannica. (My language is that of Britannia.)
Mihi opus est auceps. (My work is as a fowler.)

© Prufrock Press Inc. • *Ancient Roots and Ruins*

HANDOUT 2.3
POSSIBLE PROFESSIONS IN SLAVERY

OPUS (Work)

agaso: groom (tended to horses)

auceps: fowler (tended to chickens, pheasants, other birds)

auri custos: jewelry attendant

calator: footman

cantrix: singer

saltator: dancer

cellarius: storekeeper

coquus: cook

cursor: messenger

genus ferratile: chain gang

ianitor: doorkeeper

nuntius: messenger

pastores: shepherds

grammaticus: teacher

paedogogus: children's chaperone

vigiles: firemen

medicus: doctor

nutrix: nurse

pedisequa: attendant

sator: planter

holitor: market gardener

tonstrix: hairdresser

unctor: masseur

vestiplica: clothing folder

cistellatrix: wardrobe keeper

LESSON 3

SLAVE MARKET

Instructional Purpose: To learn about the power structure of Roman society through the eyes of the least powerful members of that society—slaves.

ACTIVITIES:

1. Ask students to complete Handout 3.1: Slavery Extended Anticipation Guide.
2. Ask students to read this page on slavery from PBS.org and complete the chart with supporting information taken from the PBS website (http://www.pbs.org/empires/romans/empire/slaves_ freemen.html).
3. Have students discuss their findings in their small groups. As they meet, they should discuss what surprised them about ancient slavery and their thoughts about modern forms of slavery, either in recent history or the present day.
4. Given all previous activities, students will write a journal entry from the perspective of their slave, focusing on a typical day in the life of a slave of that type, with that background, and at that age. Their writing should clearly illustrate an understanding of the role of slaves in ancient Rome.

HANDOUT 3.1
SLAVERY EXTENDED ANTICIPATION GUIDE

Directions: Read each statement carefully, then circle whether you think the statement is true or false. There are no wrong answers, but be prepared to have some support in mind to defend your choice.

True/False

1. Slaves were treated poorly in ancient Rome.   T   F
2. Masters never set slaves free.   T   F
3. All Roman slaves were treated the same way.   T   F
4. Only the richest households owned slaves.   T   F
5. No one sold slaves for a living—it was not very profitable.   T   F
6. Slaves that ran away faced no punishment if caught.   T   F
7. On the whole, I think I can predict what slavery is like in Rome.   T   F

Now, consult the PBS website (http://www.pbs.org/empires/romans/empire/slaves_freemen.html). What you read will either support or not support your choices on the statements above. If your reading confirms your true/false choice, put a check in the "support" blank, or if it does not, place a check in the "no support" blank. Either way, summarize the facts from the reading in your own words to the right.

	Support	No Support	Your Summary
1.			
2.			
3.			
4.			
5.			
6.			
7.			
Now summarize your opinion of slavery in Rome.			

LESSON 4

MYTHOLOGY: THE TROJAN WAR

Instructional Purpose: To explore the concept of power in war through the story of the Trojan War.

Few myths exemplify the effects of power as clearly as the story of the beginning of the Trojan War. The story details the way the gods and goddesses behave amongst each other to exert their influence and power, as well as how humans seek power through war and conquest.

ACTIVITIES:

1. According to the story, there are several characters who could be held responsible for the start of the Trojan War. Students should research the possible causes of the Trojan War by researching this list of possible culprits. For each character, state why he or she may have caused or contributed to the beginning of the Trojan War.

    *   Eris
    *   Peleus and Thetis
    *   Jupiter
    *   Venus
    *   Paris
    *   Ulysses (Odysseus)
    *   Agamemnon

2. Students should split into small groups to discuss the cause of the Trojan War. Each student should explain who is most responsible and why. As a group, they should number the characters in order of how culpable or guilty they are for starting the war. They must justify their response in a whole-class discussion.

3. Next, students will participate in a simulated PBL activity, similar to the one from Unit 2 on Roman Roads, only this time, they need to come up with a creative solution to Paris' dilemma. See the prompt below.

Situation: You are a Trojan prince and shepherd. Jupiter, the king of the gods, asks you to judge a dispute between three goddesses, one of whom must receive the golden apple labeled "to the most beautiful." Each goddess bribes you with something. Minerva, goddess of wisdom, war and technology, bribes you with military glory. Juno promises you Asia. Venus promises you the love of the most beautiful woman in the world. You have one hour to resolve this dispute without starting a war, either between humans or gods.

4. Students should work through Handout 4.1: Need to Know Board in small groups for what they must research.

5. Ask them to report their plan of action on charts. Comment and critique as a class.

6. Have students work through a secondary plan to answer the questions raised by assigning info searches to group members, deciding on the format for the project report components and the nature of their solutions.

7. Provide secondary resources for the groups to read and online websites that will assist them in their work.

8. Have students share in groups their creative resolution to the problem on the following day.

9. Ask all students to reflect on what they have learned from this PBL episode about power. How does good judgment take away the need to exert power?

HANDOUT 4.1

NEED TO KNOW BOARD

What do you know?	What do you need to know?	How are you going to find out?

© Prufrock Press Inc. • *Ancient Roots and Ruins*

LESSON 5

DEBATE

Instructional Purpose: To develop argument in oral form and to understand the connection of issues in Roman society to our own.

Another form of power in ancient Roman society was the power of persuasion through discourse, and the most powerful form of discourse was debate. This was practiced in the senate house, and more informally, in the Forum. In this lesson, students will exercise your powers of persuasion to address an important issue.

ACTIVITIES:

1. Ask students to take out their table tents and separate into groups based on the province they chose for their slave persona.
2. Ask students to form debate teams of four and prepare their debate, using one class period and time outside of class. Ask each member of the team to prepare according to the following model:
   - 1st affirmative (5 minutes)
   - 1st negative (rebuttal; 3 minutes)
   - 2nd affirmative (3 minutes)
   - Recap of overall argument (5 minutes)

3. Debate the topic of colonization in class teams, using this formal debate style.

   Proposition: Should your country have been made a colony of Rome (making all of your citizens Romans and subject to the power of Rome) or should your country have fought off the Romans, retaining local power, but at the cost of infrastructure such as much-needed roads, waterways, and public buildings?

ASSESSMENT:

Ask students to assess each debate presented according to the following criteria:

Soundness of the arguments	3	2	1
Organization of the evidence	3	2	1
Effectiveness of the delivery	3	2	1
Quality of the evidence used	3	2	1
Strengths:			
Weaknesses:			

LESSON 6

VOCABULARY LESSON: ROMAN POWER STRUCTURES

Instructional Purpose: To connect Latin words with English derivatives.

In Roman society, there were three major spheres of influence and power: the family, government, and religion. In this lesson, students will examine the vocabulary associated with all three of these spheres of influence and recognize the connections of these power structures to other languages.

ACTIVITIES:

1. Assign different pairs of students one of the list of words below. Students must look up the relevant information listed below about each word using the language website Wiktionary (http://www.wiktionary.org).
2. Each pair should complete a Vocabulary Web (p. 120) for each word from their list, giving the etymology of the word, roots and stems of that word, Latin meaning and contemporary English meaning of the word, one sentence in English using the word, and other English derivatives that use the same roots.
   - List A: domain, paternal, maternal, family, affiliation
   - List B: government, emperor, consulate, regal, council
   - List C: pope, supplicant, religion, reliquary, inauguration

3. Ask different pairs of students who did different words to share the vocabulary webs together in respect to key elements.
4. Use a projector to share student webs. Discuss the words that have the most derivatives and discuss why that might be the case.
5. Ask students to now take any three words and compare the Latin form of the word to the French, Spanish, Italian, Portuguese, and Romanian forms for it. See the sample table on page 165. Compare and contrast.

Word in Latin	French	Spanish	Italian	Portuguese	Romanian
Pater (father)					
Mater (mother)					
Pontifex (pope)					

LESSON 7

BIOGRAPHY STUDY: JULIUS CAESAR AND AUGUSTUS

Instructional Purpose: To connect the lives of famous Romans with the concept of power.

In this lesson, students will read about Julius Caesar and Augustus, two famous (and related) Roman rulers.

ACTIVITIES:

1. Have students complete Handout 7.1: Biography Chart for Julius Caesar and Augustus, consulting the following websites.
   - Wikipedia (en.wikipedia.org/wiki)
   - Encyclopedia Brittanica (http://www.britannica.com)
   - Open Library (http://www.openlibrary.org)

2. Ask the groups to report on key aspects of each life.
3. Ask students the following discussion questions.
   a. What aspects of the background of Julius Caesar and Augustus indicated what role they might assume in their societies?
   b. How did they each prepare for the roles that they assumed in society?
   c. What original contributions did each make?
   d. How important was family power and dynasty in contributing to the rise of these two great leaders? Explain.
   e. What have we learned from these biographies about the concept of power?

4. Have students write a 10-minute journal entry on a politician in our current society. Share some examples and discuss what qualities make him or her effective.
5. Now ask students to complete the comparative analysis chart on page 167 on Julius Caesar and Augustus in small groups.

	Julius Caesar	Augustus
Qualities of leadership		
Vision		
Use of symbols		
Relationships with people		
Effectiveness in war and peace		

6. Based on the chart, they should construct an argument that suggests that one or the other is the better leader of Rome. Ask student groups to share their perspectives.

HANDOUT 7.1

BIOGRAPHY CHART

Name of person:_____

Birth date and death date:_____

Family members (at birth):_____

Extended family (e.g., spouse, children):_____

_____

Early education/continued education:_____

Interests and predispositions:_____

_____

Personality characteristics:_____

_____

Abilities: _____

_____

Role he or she played in Roman history:_____

_____

_____

Contributions:_____

Important quotes (3–5):_____

_____

_____

Awards and honors:_____

Why is he or she still remembered today?_____

_____

_____

LESSON 8

INTERDISCIPLINARY LESSON: ART AND ARCHITECTURE OF POWER

Instructional Purpose: To examine how power is communicated through art and architecture.

Roman rulers, particularly Augustus, used monumental works of art and architecture to shape their image and portray the power of Rome. In this lesson, students will explore how selected works portray the concept of power and will create their own powerful portrait of Julius Caesar.

ACTIVITIES:

1. Project an image of Augustus to the front of the room or give each student a copy of the image.
2. Ask each student to write a free-response essay for 30 minutes on this prompt: How does this art piece project the power of Rome through the depiction of Augustus?
3. Following their free writing, lead a whole-group discussion, particularly noting what characteristics of this art piece students pick up on.
4. Individually, ask students to view images of Augustus online and choose a second image to answer the following questions.
   a. How does the artist idealize the figure of Augustus in this portrayal?
   b. What commonalities do you see in the two images of Augustus? What differences do you see?
   c. Which depiction proves the more effective in conveying a sense of Roman power? Why?

5. Ask students to sketch their own depiction of Julius Caesar, based on their work with the image of Augustus. In the image, have students label the specific ways they have conveyed his power. Ask students to share the results with small groups.
6. Teachers may exhibit the images of Julius Caesar created by students.

LESSON 9

LITERARY POWER

Instructional Purpose: To examine how power is communicated through words.

Roman leaders also expressed their power through literary works. Julius Caesar, in his *De Bello Gallico*, portrays his efforts in Gaul and the might of the Roman empire, and Vergil, in the *Aeneid*, places Augustus at the center of the affairs of gods and men in the ancient world. Contemporary authors celebrated the successes of both men during their lives and in their eulogies. Even after their deaths, the message of power lives on in the writings students will examine.

ACTIVITIES:

1. Ask students to read the following inscription, one of Augustus' eulogies.

    > [The Most Divine Caesar] has reestablished a Universe that had everywhere been in disintegration and had degenerated into a lamentable state. He has put a new face on the whole cosmos . . . Providence has . . . [brought] life to perfection in producing Augustus— whom it has filled with virtue to be the benefactor of Mankind, sending him to us and to posterity as a savior whose mission has been to put an end to war and to set the Universe in order. (Inscription, probable date 9 BCE; text as in Dittenberger, 1905)

2. Have students respond to this inscription individually by answering the following questions in free-response form.
    a. According to this inscription, what gives Augustus lasting power and influence on the world?
    b. Based on your research from the biography lesson, do you think this inscription is justified? Why or why not?

3. Ask students to read the following passage from Plutarch.

At the time of his death Caesar was fully 56 years old, but he had survived Pompey not much more than four years, while of the power and dominion which he had sought all his life at so great risks, and barely achieved at last, of this he had reaped no fruit but the name of it only, and a glory which had awakened envy on the part of his fellow citizens. However, the great guardian-genius of the man, whose help he had enjoyed through life, followed upon him even after death as an avenger of his murder, driving and tracking down his slayers over every land and sea until not one of them was left, but even those who in any way soever either put hand to the deed or took part in the plot were punished. (Plutarch, 1929)

4. Have students respond to this inscription individually by answering the following questions in free-response form.
   a. According to this inscription, what gives Julius Caesar lasting power and influence on the world?
   b. Based on your research from the biography lesson, do you think this perspective is justified? Why or why not?

5. Now ask students to compare the two passages. What tone does each convey? What is the same or different about the two messages? Do they reflect different values, or are the Roman values celebrated in each fundamentally the same?

REFERENCES

Dittenberger, W. (Ed.). (1905). *Orientis Graeci inscriptiones selectae.* Leipzig, Germany: Herzel.

Plutarch (1929). *The parallel lives* (B. Perrin, Trans.). London, England: Loeb Classical Library.

LESSON 10

PERSUASION

Instructional Purpose: To connect ancient messages about power with modern propaganda techniques.

In the last two lessons, students have examined how leaders communicate power through visual and written media. In the modern world, new technology provides new forms for these messages. In this lesson, students will create their own advertisement to market the greatness of Rome to a current audience.

ACTIVITIES:

1. Have students review the forms of propaganda studied in Lessons 8 and 9. In small groups, have them discuss what forms propaganda takes in the modern world—are they still the same? Different? If so, how?

2. Ask students to share and list forms of propaganda in the modern world in a whole-class discussion.

3. Using modern advertising (especially SuperBowl commercials) as a model, ask students to create their own high-powered video ad promoting Roman power, one that persuades a modern audience that ancient Rome was and is a great power. See Handout 10.1: Evaluation of Video Project for a grading rubric.

HANDOUT 10.1
EVALUATION OF VIDEO PROJECT

Each category can earn you up to 6 points. An average score will determine your grade for this project. The stated criteria represent a score of 6.

CONTENT	
• You present a clear and compelling message to your intended audience. • You demonstrate effective research skills by including relevant, reliable information in your message. • You create and select images that convey meaning and purpose to support your message.	_____ out of 6 points
ORGANIZATION	
• You demonstrated careful planning and team cooperation during this process. • You sequence your message to communicate effectively.	_____ out of 6 points
VOICE	
• You establish and maintain a point of view and apply a unique style to your video that matches the audience and subject matter.	_____ out of 6 points
LANGUAGE USE	
• You choose words that have impact and precision. Your language has been edited for serious errors of grammar, sentence structure, and conventions. Your language flows naturally and enhances your message.	_____ out of 6 points
USE OF TECHNOLOGY	
• You demonstrate skill in using the application(s) required for this project. Your final product has obviously been screened, revised, and edited to ensure that technical issues do not detract from your message. • You master the technology, not vice-versa.	_____ out of 6 points
PRESENTATION	
• Your product fulfills the assignment specifications for length and format. You turned in all of the required documents and include necessary source information.	_____ out of 6 points
Average Score:	

© Prufrock Press Inc. • *Ancient Roots and Ruins*

UNIT ASSESSMENT

PERSUASIVE ESSAY PROMPT

Do the ends justify the means: Should Roman leaders have exerted power in the ways that they did in order to build empire?

RESOURCES

http://www.pbs.org/empires/romans/empire/slaves_freemen.html

http://en.wikipedia.org/wiki

http://www.britannica.com

http://www.openlibrary.org

http://www.wiktionary.org

Dittenberger, W. (Ed.). (1905). Orientis Graeci Inscriptiones Selectae. Leipzig, Germany: Herzel.

Plutarch (1929). The parallel lives (B. Terrin, Trans.). London, England: Loeb Classical Library.

UNIT 4

INNOVATION

> *Tempora mutantur, et nos mutamur in illis.*
> The times are changed; even we are changed in them.
> —Ovid, *The Metamorphoses*

CONCEPT OF INNOVATION

In studying ancient civilizations, people today often see much in what these civilizations produced and think current-day ideas are merely derivatives of what was already considered at that time. In this unit, students will explore how the Romans were innovators in their own time and built extensively on the ideas of others to improve their society.

KEY GENERALIZATIONS

» Innovation is adapting others' ideas to meet societal needs.
» Innovation requires problem solving and flexible thinking.

» Innovation is product-based.
» Innovation depends on the productive reflection and application of the creativity of others.

ESSENTIAL QUESTIONS

» Why is innovation as important as creativity to the advancement of a civilization?
» How did Roman innovation increase the influence of the Empire?
» What innovations of the Romans are still in use today?

GOALS AND OUTCOMES

» Develop an understanding of Roman innovations through the study of historical artifacts.

Students will be able to:
- analyze Roman contributions to extract meaning, and
- synthesize Roman ideas by modeling selected language features in selected genres.

» Develop an understanding of key concepts that underlie Roman civilization.

Students will be able to:
- analyze the language of Latin through vocabulary and grammar,
- evaluate Roman engineering principles, and
- develop relevant products that apply Roman innovation.

» Develop critical thinking and reasoning.

Students will be able to:
- design arguments to support a given perspective on Roman thoughts and products, and
- evaluate the contribution of Roman innovations in language and engineering to the history of the world.

» Express creative ideas in multiple forms.

Students will be able to:

- create written and visual products that express ideas about key concepts, and
- synthesize multiple forms to create a montage of Roman contributions.

LESSON 1

INTRODUCTION TO THE UNIT

> *Nil novi sub sole.*
> There is nothing new under the sun.

Instructional Purpose: To introduce students to the concept of innovation.

ACTIVITIES:

1. Place students in groups of 3–5 and ask them to name as many people as they can who have invented something that has improved American society. They should try to list at least 15 people.
2. Have students make their lists on chart paper and share the examples by group. As each group adds new examples, the teacher should generate a master chart of names.
3. Groups should categorize the domains in which their inventors have contributed. Ask students to share their categories by groups. Create a master list of the domains of invention generated. Ask students why some categories have several but others have so few.
4. Ask students for some examples of human qualities needed to perform in these domains. Discuss a few and write them on the master list.
5. Have students list nonexamples (people who are not exemplary of having creative or innovative qualities). Once they are finished brainstorming, have the groups share their examples. Make a master list.
6. Ask: What do these people have in common? What qualities do you think keep them from being creative or innovative? Discuss as a whole class.
7. Instruct the groups to generate 2–3 generalizations about innovation. Ask: How do these generalizations apply to all of your examples and none of your nonexamples?
8. Ask students to contribute their generalizations to the master chart. Do they all fit the people generated as examples?

9. In their groups, ask students to review their list of generalizations, as well as the unit generalizations, and do the following.
   a. Indicate which ones from their list are close to the ones found in the unit.
   b. Decide which unit generalizations apply to examples of people the group generated.
   c. Determine which generalizations do not fit the work done thus far.

10. Tell students that both sets of generalizations will guide their understanding of the concept of creativity and innovation better as they explore it through studying the innovations of the Romans.

11. Now ask students to generate a list of creative and innovative qualities that they consider important based on their work. Have each group share its list and create a master list for reference during the unit.

12. Ask students to choose one quality of creativity and innovation and write a one-paragraph argument supporting its importance for all leaders. (Allow 15 minutes.)

13. Ask students to share 3–5 examples orally. Have students begin a portfolio of their writing for use during the unit and include this piece as their first entry.

ASSESSMENT:

Teachers should use the constructed work of students as the basis for judging their initial understanding of the concept of innovation. Keep student work around the room as baseline for their work in the unit.

LESSON 2

INNOVATION MYTHS: THE LESSON OF ICARUS

Instructional Purpose: To demonstrate how innovation and creativity were employed by the gods and mimicked by men in ancient times.

The gods and goddesses were always inventing and creating. Because they were all related, they also took ideas and products from each other to serve their own ends, demonstrating that the creative ideas that are best are often those that are put to good use by others.

For example, the lyre, invented by Mercury, was taken and played by Apollo, even becoming one of his symbols. The flute, invented by Minerva, was played by the forest god Pan.

ACTIVITIES:

1. Ask students to read a version of the Daedalus and Icarus myth from an online source or from Edith Hamilton's or Bulfinch's mythology collections.

2. Discuss the following questions about the myth with the whole class.
   a. Why did ancient man need a myth like this one?
   b. What purposes did this story fulfill? What was its moral for the Greeks and Romans?
   c. What pattern does the myth follow?
   d. What aspects of human behavior does the myth demonstrate?
   e. Icarus tries out the wings that his father Daedalus created that eventually are responsible for his demise. What aspects of being creative or innovative are being explored here? What lessons are learned?
   f. What lessons are revealed about fathers and sons?

3. Have students read Handout 2.1: William Carlos Williams Poem. While they are reading the poem, project the Bruegel painting, "Landscape with the Fall of Icarus," on a screen for them to view.

4. In small groups, have students analyze the painting and the poem in relationship to the myth. Ask the following questions regarding the painting.
   a. What do you see in the painting that relates to the myth?
   b. What important ideas from the myth are portrayed?
   c. What images and symbols does Bruegel employ?
   d. What is the structure of the painting? How is it organized?
   e. What feelings does the painting produce in you as the viewer?

5. Ask the following questions regarding the poem.
   a. What words are important in conveying the tone of the poem?
   b. What images that Williams uses are the most powerful? Why?
   c. What is the theme of this poem?
   d. How do you react to it?
   e. What structural devices does Williams use to heighten the impact of his poem?

6. Ask the following questions regarding the comparison of myth, picture, and poem.
   a. How do Williams and Bruegel each interpret the myth? Are there distinctions in their interpretation?
   b. How does each artist extend the myth for the audience of his time?
   c. Both the writer and the painter were working in innovative forms in their art when they did these works. What aspects of creativity do you see in each product? Read about Bruegel and Williams in respect to their work.

FOLLOW-UP PROJECT:

Have students select a Roman myth of their choice and create a poem and illustration that depicts that myth. Have them write an artist's statement about key aspects of interpretation (i.e., theme, vocabulary, structure, images and symbols). Student products should be judged according to the following criteria:

Interpretation of the myth selected in both words and images	5	4	3	2	1
Quality of the products	5	4	3	2	1
Use of creative and innovative ideas	5	4	3	2	1
Use of effective images in both the poem and the illustration	5	4	3	2	1
Effective discussion of artistic elements employed	5	4	3	2	1
Command of language mechanics (i.e., spelling, grammar, and usage)	5	4	3	2	1

HANDOUT 2.1

WILLIAM CARLOS WILLIAMS POEM

Landscape with the Fall of Icarus
William Carlos Williams

According to Brueghel
when Icarus fell
it was spring

a farmer was ploughing
his field
the whole pageantry

of the year was
awake tingling
near

the edge of the sea
concerned
with itself

sweating in the sun
that melted
the wings' wax

unsignificantly
off the coast
there was

a splash quite unnoticed
this was
Icarus drowning

LESSON 3

LANGUAGE INNOVATION THROUGH VOCABULARY

Instructional Purpose: To engage students in understanding how English words are rooted in Latin.

The Romans invented the Latin language, which has influenced English in a number of ways. In this lesson, students will see how it has impacted the vocabulary used in English by studying words that have Latin roots and relate to the concept of this unit.

ACTIVITIES:

1. Ask students to do a Vocabulary Web (see Handout 3.1) of the following words in English:
   a. Innovate
   b. Create
   c. Invent
   d. Improvise
   e. Dedicate
   f. Contemplate

2. The web should address the following components:
   a. definition of the word;
   b. word stems, their meanings, and their origins;
   c. word families or derivatives (What other words in English employ these same stems?);
   d. part of speech;
   e. aynonyms and antonyms; and
   f. application of all six words in an original paragraph.

3. Students should share their Vocabulary Web and paragraph in small groups. Ask several students to share with the total group.

ASSESSMENT:

Students turn in their webs for teacher assessment on the criteria of completeness, accuracy, and number of derivatives.

HANDOUT 3.1

VOCABULARY WEB

Vocabulary Web

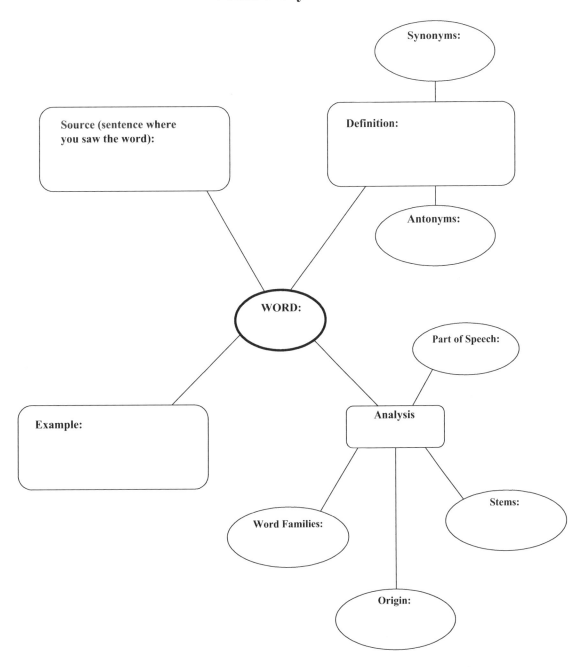

LESSON 4

LANGUAGE INNOVATION THROUGH GRAMMAR

Instructional Purpose: To analyze English sentences according to forms and functions of words.

Both English and Latin define word relationships in distinctive ways. Both languages have four levels on which we can analyze grammar in sentences and two ways we can classify sentences as patterns.

The four levels are:
- **Parts of speech:** nouns, pronouns, verbs, adjectives, adverbs, conjunctions, interjections, prepositions.

- **Parts of a sentence:** subject and predicate; for example, The armies (subject) clashed by night (predicate).

- **Phrases:** groups of words used together as a collective without a subject or predicate but connected to a main sentence; for example, The charming girls *from the city of Bath* congregated *in the atrium.*

- **Clauses:** a group of words with a subject and predicate but connected to a main sentence; for example, *When he had finished writing his book*, Vergil put his pen down and sighed with relief.

The two sentence patterns are:
- Three different types of sentences (declarative, interrogative, imperative) and
- Three different levels of complexity (simple, compound, and complex)

Examples of sentence patterns include:
- Sara, please bring me the mail so that I can check my stocks. (imperative and complex)

- Why must we always be fighting over small things? (interrogative and simple)
- You have a long day ahead of you, and we must load the car in preparation. (declarative and compound)

ACTIVITIES:

1. Ask students to analyze the following sentences about mythology according to the levels and types of grammar explained above.
   a. Myth is an attempt to narrate a whole human experience, of which the purpose is too deep, going too deep in the blood and soul, for mental explanation or description.—D. H. Lawrence
   b. The depth of your mythology is the extent of your effectiveness.—John C. Maxwell
   c. It is a myth, not a mandate, a fable not a logic, and symbol rather than reason by which men are moved.—Irwin Edman
   d. Myths which are believed in tend to become true.—George Orwell

2. Use Handout 4.1: Myth Analysis to have students complete the analysis.
3. Share results using a Smart Board.
4. For each lesson following this one, ask students to analyze a sentence from one of the readings in a similar fashion.
5. Ask students to group themselves with a partner who analyzed the same statement. Paraphrase what each statement means and why it would be stated by the author.
6. Ask one group who dealt with each statement to report to the class. Arrive at a common understanding of each myth statement and who the authors were.
7. Challenge question: How does knowing the grammar of a sentence help us understand the meaning of a sentence better? Ask students to discuss for 5 minutes in small groups and then discuss as a class.

HANDOUT 4.1

MYTH ANALYSIS

Parts of speech used:

_____

_____

Parts of the sentence:

_____

_____

Phrases:

_____

_____

Clauses:

_____

_____

Sentence type (declarative, interrogative, imperative):

_____

_____

Sentence pattern (simple, compound, complex):

_____

_____

What do you think the author is saying about the concept of myth? Why would he be saying it?

_____

_____

_____

LESSON 5

BIOGRAPHY LESSON ON ROMAN WRITERS: VERGIL AND OVID

Instructional Purpose: To develop an understanding of the lives and works of Rome's greatest poets.

In this lesson, students will read about Vergil and Ovid, two famous writers from the Golden Age of Rome.

ACTIVITIES:

1. Have students complete Handout 5.1: Biography Chart for Vergil and Ovid, consulting the following websites.
   - Wikipedia (en.wikipedia.org/wiki)
   - Encyclopedia Brittanica (http://www.britannica.com)
   - Open Library (http://www.openlibrary.org)

2. Ask the groups to report on key aspects of each life.
3. Ask students the following discussion questions.
   a. What aspects of the background of each poet indicated what role he might assume in his society?
   b. What personality characteristics contributed to their success or lack thereof in Roman society?
   c. What original contributions did each make?
   d. How important were the times in which they lived in explaining their ability to make a living as poets?
   e. What have we learned from these biographies about the concept of innovation?

4. Have students write a 10-minute journal entry on the role of innovation in any society. Share some examples and discuss.
5. Now ask students to complete a comparative analysis chart on Vergil and Ovid in small groups using the one on page 190.

	Vergil	Ovid
Forms of writing (i.e., style, subject matter, devices)		
Use of symbols and imagery		
How they appeal to the reader		

6. Based on the chart, construct an argument that suggests that one or the other is the better poet in posterity. Ask student groups to share their perspectives.

HANDOUT 5.1

BIOGRAPHY CHART

Name of person: _____

Birth date and death date: _____

Family members (at birth): _____

Extended family (e.g., spouse, children): _____

Early education/continued education: _____

Interests and predispositions: _____

_____

Personality characteristics: _____

_____

Abilities: _____

_____

Role he or she played in Roman history: _____

_____

_____

Contributions: _____

Important quotes (3–5): _____

_____

_____

Awards and honors: _____

Is your person an innovator or creator? Explain. _____

Why is he or she still remembered today? _____

_____

_____

LESSON 6

THE ROLE OF ROMAN THEATER IN CULTURE

Instructional Purpose: To examine theater in ancient Rome as an innovation.

The Roman theatre, while similar in many ways to its Greek predecessor, had several distinctive features and playwrights who went beyond dramatic and comedic forms used by the Greeks. Although the Greeks invented theatre, the Romans innovated on their use of forms, both physical and literary, particularly when it came to comedy.

The Greeks invented the amphitheatre, or "theatre in the round" as we might call it today. The Romans added to the form and recreated buildings of striking similarity with small but important differences.

ACTIVITIES:

1. Find and examine online images of the Theatre of Ephesus (in modern-day Turkey) and the Theatre of Arausio (in modern-day Orange, France). Both theatres have been called technical marvels due to their incredible acoustics—a clap onstage can be heard clearly all the way in the back row. What features do both stages share? What differences do you see between them? How would you describe these differences?

2. Read the Greek Theatre and Roman Theatre sections on this website (http://www3.northern.edu/wild/th100/CHAPT11.HTM) and answer the following questions.
    a. What differences do the authors of this website see between Greek and Roman theatre?
    b. How do they compare to the differences you listed?
    c. Why do you think Roman architects changed the form of the physical theatres?

3. The two foremost Roman playwrights whose works survive, Plautus and Terence, stole most of their plots from the Greek

Menander, although most would agree the Roman authors made Menander's stock characters funnier. Read a description of Plautus' typical stock characters at the Vassar website (http://faculty.vassar.edu/jolott/old_courses/republic1998/plautus/stockcharacters.html).

4. Reflect on modern comedies. What typical or stock personality types do you see often in sitcoms and movie comedies? Why do you think these traits appear so often on screen?

5. In ancient theatre, stock characters were easily visible to the audience because they wore specific masks that illustrated clearly the age of the character, if they were happy or sad, and other characteristics (e.g., rosy cheeks, bruises, a sarcastic smirk, etc.) Read through the timeline of Roman theatre and theatrical masks at this website (http://www.arlymasks.com/timeline.htm).

6. Pick any three masks illustrated in the timeline from Greco-Roman theatre, then answer the following questions.
   a. Does this mask reflect a stereotype or stock character that is recognizable to you?
   b. How did the artist convey the personality of the character in the mask?
   c. What could be changed to make the mask more specific?

7. Using construction paper, have students create a Roman theatrical mask for a kind of "stock character" seen today, either on television or in movies. Their masks should clearly illustrate a specific set of personality traits that would be understood by their audience.

8. Have students create a short monologue to give, using their masks to represent the characters they are portraying. Have a few students share their monologues and discuss the effectiveness of the mask in understanding the character and his or her traits.

9. In both Greek and Roman theater, the audience's reaction was a major consideration of playwrights. Tragedy would produce strong identification with the play and its characters, creating a state of catharsis in the audience. In comedy, the reaction would be laughter, emanating from the visual puns, slapstick movements of the characters, and the ridiculousness of the situation. Discuss the following questions with students.

a. What role do you think theater played in Roman life, given the lack of television, radio, and other modes of modern-day communication and depiction?

b. What is the role of theater in today's culture? Has the importance of tragedy and comedy changed? Why do you think so?

10. Have students create a journal entry that summarizes their understanding of the importance of Roman theater in ancient times. Ask 3–4 students to read their entry. Discuss as appropriate.

11. Some students may want to create a more formalized Roman theatre mask. If they are interested, refer them to this website and process (http://www.ehow.com/how_12204258_make-roman-theater-mask.html).

LESSON 7

THE ARCH

Instructional Purpose: To design structures using Roman technology.

The engineering marvels of the Romans are still considered amazing today because many of their building feats are still standing in Italy and in the provinces, including England. Students will have the opportunity in this lesson to create a model of one of these structural feats and understand the principles by which it was constructed.

ACTIVITIES:

1. Have students read about the importance of the arch in engineering, especially in building bridges. *On the Water-Management of the City of Rome* by Sextus Julius Frontinus (http://www.uvm.edu/~rrodgers/Frontinus.html) is a good primary source; secondary sources include the Gazetteer (http://penelope.uchicago.edu/Thayer/E/Gazetteer/Periods/Roman/Topics/Engineering/waterworks) and How Stuff Works (http://www.howstuffworks.com/engineering/structural/10-roman-engineering-tricks.htm#page=2).

2. Discuss the following questions.
   a. Why was the arch so important to the Roman building program?
   b. How did the arch contribute to upgrading the quality of Roman life? life in the provinces?
   c. What was innovative about the structure in respect to how Romans used it?

3. Ask students to read the Encyclopedia Brittanica entry for Appius Claudius Caecus, a famous aqueduct and road builder. You might also direct them to English translations of Roman writers who mention him, such as Sextus Julius Frontinus' *The Aqueducts of Rome*, section i.5 (http://penelope.uchicago.edu/Thayer/E/Roman/Texts/Frontinus/De_Aquis/text*.html) or Diodorus Siculus' Bibliotheca Historia, section xx.36 (http://penelope.uchicago.edu/Thayer/E/Roman/Texts/Diodorus_Siculus/20B*.

html). What innovations did he make to improve transportation of people, goods, and water at the time?

4. Ask students to select one of the following innovations used by the Romans and create a model of it, using appropriate scale measurement. They can use Handout 7.2: Plan for Construction of a Roman Structure Artifact to plan their construction. Assess using Handout 7.1: Product Assessment Rubric.
   a. aqueduct
   b. Appian Way
   c. catapult
   d. triumphal arch

5. Have students label the parts and explain how the mechanism worked. Then have them write a statement describing its impact on Roman life or the conduct of war on transportation of goods or all three.

6. Display the student work as exhibits. Ask students to judge the top three and ask those students to present their work for the class.

HANDOUT 7.1

PRODUCT ASSESSMENT RUBRIC

The models will be assessed by students and the teacher on the following criteria scale.

Use of scale	5	4	3	2	1
Creative use of materials	5	4	3	2	1
Description of the innovation in labeling and narrative	5	4	3	2	1
Statement of impact	5	4	3	2	1
Strengths:					
Weaknesses:					

NAME: _____ DATE: _____

HANDOUT 7.2

PLAN FOR CONSTRUCTION OF A ROMAN STRUCTURE ARTIFACT

Problem/project for construction:_____

_____

_____

_____

Brainstormed solutions:_____

_____

_____

_____

Materials needed:_____

_____

Problems with development:_____

_____

_____

My solutions:_____

_____

_____

Purpose of my product:_____

_____

_____

Special features:_____

_____

_____

© Prufrock Press Inc. • *Ancient Roots and Ruins*

LESSON 8

MILITARY INNOVATION

Instructional Purpose: To analyze the military innovations introduced by Caesar and Hannibal.

In the last lesson, students worked with engineering innovations that changed the way the Romans lived and the structures they inhabited. In this lesson, they will consider the role of military innovations in the successful campaigns waged by the two top generals—Caesar and Hannibal.

ACTIVITIES:

1. Have students read selected website material on Caesar's strategies used in the Gallic Wars and other forays before his crossing of the Rubicon.
2. Then have students create a concept map that illustrates the innovations he employed in the pursuit of war.
3. Now have the students read about the military prowess of Hannibal in his exploits in the Alps. Ask them to add to their innovations maps, based on what they have learned.
4. Assign the students an argumentative paper to write in class (30 minutes) that responds to the following prompt: Roman generals employed innovative techniques of war that resulted in successful conquests of new territory. Assess using Handout 8.1: Persuasive Writing Rubric.
5. Share a few example papers and lead a discussion in the class about the tactics used in Roman conflict.
    a. How much of Roman success was due to their weapons technology and how much to their psychological insights about war?
    b. What military advantages did the Romans enjoy in many of the battles you read about?
    c. What disadvantages did the Romans have to deal with in their conflicts?
    d. Based on your readings to date, what factors would you identify as most important in Rome's becoming the major power of the ancient world?

6. To conclude this lesson, ask students to create a metaphor that captures Roman innovation. Share in small groups and display in the room.

HANDOUT 8.1

PERSUASIVE WRITING RUBRIC

	0	2	4	6	8
Claim or Opinion	No clear position exists on the writer's assertion, preference, or view, and context does not help to clarify it.	Writer's position is poorly formulated, but reader is reasonably sure what the paper is about based on context	A clear topic sentence exists, and the reader is reasonably sure what the paper is about based on the strength of the topic sentence alone.	A very clear, concise position is given and position is elaborated with reference to reasons; multiple sentences are used to form the claim. Must include details that explain the context	n/a
Data or Supporting Point	No reasons are offered that are relevant to the claim.	One or two weak reasons are offered; the reasons are relevant to the claim	At least two strong reasons are offered that are relevant to the claim.	At least three reasons are offered that are relevant to the claim.	At least three reasons are offered that are also accurate, convincing, and distinct.
Elaboration	No elaboration is provided.	An attempt is made to elaborate at least one reason.	More than one reason is supported with relevant details.	Each reason (three) is supported with relevant information that is clearly connected to the claim.	The writer explains all reasons in a very effective, convincing, multi paragraph structure.
Conclusion	No conclusion/ closing sentence is provided.	A conclusion/ closing sentence is provided.	A conclusion is provided that revisits the main ideas.	A strong concluding paragraph is provided that revisits and summarizes main ideas.	n/a

HANDOUT 8.1, CONTINUED

Praise, Ideas, Suggestions: _____

_____

_____

_____

_____

_____

_____

_____

_____

_____

_____

_____

_____

_____

_____

_____

_____

_____

_____

_____

_____

_____

LESSON 9

LAW AND GOVERNMENT

Instructional Purpose: To compare Roman ideas of law, order, and justice to our own.

Often, historians have claimed that our system of government as a representational democracy is based on the Roman model, that our legal system is indebted to the Romans, and that our sense of justice is similar to theirs as well. (It is also appropriate to note that our current systems of governance also owe much to the Enlightenment models of the 18th century). In this lesson, students will explore the history of the Roman Republic and its systems of governance and compare it to the United States' systems.

ACTIVITIES:

1. Ask students to read historical accounts of the way that government functioned in Rome. Then have them read about Roman law and the society's system of jurisprudence. They can use the resources at Fordham University (http://www.fordham.edu/halsall/ancient/12tables.asp), Lacus Curtius (http://penelope.uchicago.edu/Thayer/E/Roman/Texts/secondary/SMIGRA/Law/home.html), and the Latin Law Library (http://webu2.upmf-grenoble.fr/DroitRomain/).

2. Conduct a class discussion, using the following questions in a Socratic seminar model.
   a. What was the organizational structure of the Roman Republic? How did that structure allow for checks and balances of power?
   b. What assumptions did the Romans make about justice, as seen in their gladiatorial combats, their system of deciding guilt or innocence, and their writings about the need for societal control?
   c. How did the military control reward and punishment in Roman society?
   d. How did the systems change under the emperors, beginning with Augustus?

3. Now ask students to work in small groups to complete Handout 9.1: Comparative Analysis Chart that illustrates similarities and differences in the governmental systems of Rome and the United States today.

4. After students have completed their charts, ask them to report out their findings. Create a class comparison chart.

5. Conclude the lesson by discussing the following questions with the whole class.

   a. How does a system of government dictate the nature of justice within a society?

   b. Has American representative democracy proven to be effective in its safeguards for guaranteeing justice for all citizens? Why or why not?

ASSESSMENT:

Teachers should informally monitor the group work, ensuring that students are engaged in analyzing the two systems.

NAME: _____ DATE: _____

HANDOUT 9.1

COMPARATIVE ANALYSIS CHART

Governmental Systems	Rome (Republic)	United States
Executive		
Legislative		
Judicial		
Legal		
Military		
Citizen Rights		

LESSON 10

DEBATE

Instructional Purpose: To develop argument in oral form and understand the connection of issues in Roman society to our own.

The Romans developed the debate form of oratory to the highest level as a regular part of their civil discourse and used it with regularity in daily life in the Forum and elsewhere. In this lesson, students will experience the format used by Cicero and Cato and other orators and politicians in Rome during the Republic to debate an issue they would have debated as well.

ACTIVITIES:

1. Ask students to form debate teams of four and prepare their debate, using one class period and time outside of class. Ask each member of the team to prepare according to the following model:
   - 1st affirmative (5 minutes)
   - 1st negative (rebuttal; 3 minutes)
   - 2nd affirmative (3 minutes)
   - Recap of overall argument (5 minutes)

2. Debate the topic of taxation in class teams using this formal debate style.

   Proposition: In times of economic trouble, should the state tax citizens to help the economy, or should the state give citizens more money to spend to stimulate growth?

3. After the debate presentations, ask students to consider the following questions.
   a. What similarities and differences do you see in the issues of Roman society and our own?
   b. How does the issue of taxation impact the overall health of a society? Explain.

c. Who benefits and who is harmed by using taxation as a solution to the economic problems of a state? Try to reach consensus on the role of taxation in a society.

ASSESSMENT:

Ask students to assess each debate presented according to the following criteria:

Soundness of the arguments	3	2	1
Organization of the evidence	3	2	1
Effectiveness of the delivery	3	2	1
Quality of the evidence used	3	2	1
Strengths:			
Weaknesses:			

UNIT ASSESSMENT

Allow one period of 40 minutes for an essay to be completed. Give students this prompt:

- Develop an argument that contends the following: Roman innovation remains as a model for our modern world.
- Be sure to state your opinion, support it with at least three examples that you elaborate on, and include a conclusion.

The rubric to be used for assessing the unit essay may be found in Handout 8.1: Persuasive Writing Rubric.

UNIT 5

EXPRESSION

> *Exegi monumentum aere perennius.*
> I have built a monument more lasting than bronze.
>
> —Horace

CONCEPT OF ROMAN EXPRESSION

We know the Romans through their arts. The story of Pompeii is written in red in their expansive wall murals. The history of Rome and Roman values are alluded to in the *Aeneid.* Roman philosophy and virtues are seen in Horace's *Odes.* The various forms of expression used in Rome over the centuries ranged from epic literature to lyric (love) poetry to plays. In the visual arts, painting, sculpture, and mosaics predominated. Music was adapted from Greek tones to new instruments, and singers added new lyrics in the vocabulary of spoken stories.

The ancient Hebrews in writing the Old Testament were among the first people to lay out the central tenets and stories of their religion in codified (or written) form. Their writings focused on God's works of creation, his wrath, his mercy, and his covenant with the Jewish people.

Although written by many authors, the Old Testament presented a single theme of human destiny linked to the divine.

The ancient Greeks used heroic myths as their sacred texts to define not their past, but their future. These were the tales of men, not gods, who questioned their moral purpose in the world. In myth (literally "word" in Greek), people learn of ancient times beyond everyday experience, through a world of superhuman creatures, wondrous events and miracles. Having no known author, they survived through oral traditions of song and speech, communicated by ancient bards (singing storytellers). Of particular merit were the Homeric myths associated ultimately with the *Iliad* and the *Odyssey*, tales of heroes of the Trojan War and the adventures of Odysseus respectively.

The ancient Romans evolved sacred text in the same way as the Greeks—through stories about human fears assuaged by the gods, those same gods of the Greeks renamed. They also created their own heroic myth in the form of the *Aeneid*, a story of the founding of Rome from the ashes of Troy. This heroic myth became the basis of Roman education and of many important works of English poetry as well. As such, myth became literature as it celebrated the spread of Rome's grandeur and the deeds of its emperor Augustus.

KEY GENERALIZATIONS

» Expression of ideas through various forms of art tells the story of a civilization.
» Expression in form is a means to communicate the philosophy, history, and religion of a culture and its people.
» Expression provides a way to articulate meaning for both individuals and groups within a society.

ESSENTIAL QUESTIONS

» What Roman forms of expression still communicate meaning for our lives today?
» How have art forms of expression (i.e., painting, literature, theater, architecture) changed to reflect different societal values and beliefs?

» What beliefs do our expressive arts reflect about our society today? How does this vary by our cultural backgrounds and experiences?

GOALS AND OUTCOMES

» Develop an understanding of Roman cultural values and beliefs through the study of artistic artifacts.

Students will be able to:
- analyze Roman visual and textual products to extract meaning; and
- synthesize Roman ideas by modeling selected product styles.

» Develop an understanding of key concepts that underlie Roman civilization.

Students will be able to:
- analyze ancient Roman texts,
- evaluate Roman art forms and styles, and
- develop relevant products that use Roman concepts.

» Develop critical thinking and reasoning.

Students will be able to:
- design arguments to support a given perspective of a Roman belief, and
- evaluate the contribution of the Roman art forms to the history of the world.

» Express creative ideas in multiple forms.

Students will be able to:
- create written and visual products that express ideas about key concepts, and
- synthesize multiple forms to create a montage of text and images.

LESSON 1

INTRODUCTION TO THE UNIT

Instructional Purpose: To introduce the concept of expression found in Roman culture.

The prevalence of remaining Roman artifacts allows us to understand firsthand their importance to the culture in which they were created. In this lesson, students will study selected artifacts to learn more deeply about their significance and role in Roman society.

ACTIVITIES:

1. Ask students to examine the following 8 artifacts in slide form and answer the questions posed about each.
   a. bust of Augustus
   b. a Horatian Ode
   c. The Pont du Gard
   d. Ara Pacis
   e. the Trevi Fountain in Rome
   f. the Roman Forum
   g. the Roman theater at Orange, France
   h. Venus de Milo sculpture

2. Ask students the following discussion questions.
   a. What do you see in the artifact? Describe it.
   b. What ideas does it convey? How?
   c. What clues does it provide to some facet of Roman life?
   d. What does it communicate to you about Roman life, customs, and beliefs?

3. Ask students to share their impressions in small groups.
4. Introduce the unit's generalizations about expression and provide more detailed commentary on each of the artifacts the students have examined.
5. Explain that we know ancient civilizations by what they have left behind. The study of archaeology is the uncovering of artifacts that reveal important clues to these civilizations. For contemporary

Western civilizations, the study of Roman civilization gives us the basis of our laws, our customs, and many of our values and beliefs. It also has influenced our art, literature, and philosophy. Even our strategies of war owe much to those of the Romans.

6. Ask students to find and bring to class examples of Roman civilization or the Latin language visible to us today. Provide time for them to share these examples on each day of the unit.

LESSON 2

TESSELATIONS

Instructional Purpose: To demonstrate ideas by modeling a Roman artistic form and to apply mathematical patterning to art.

Tessellations are a patterned art form that employs geometric shapes in a tight design, used by the Romans in many decorative arts. They were most often seen in mosaics, although they could be found in pottery and wall painting as well. The use of tessellations reached a high level in the work of M. C. Escher, a mathematician and artist of the 20th century. In anticipation of this lesson, go to the Tessellations website (http://www.tessellations.org) and have students review the examples provided. They should read about Escher and examine his work on the website. Also have them visit tessellation images on Google. In this lesson, students will create their own tessellations and apply them to an original mosaic.

ACTIVITIES:

1. Ask students to create a tessellation that represents a key Roman concept such as myth, paganism, democracy, or duty. Provide materials or have them do one online at the designated website above. They may want to limit the size of the tessellation to one tile that measures 12" by 12".

2. Have students present their tessellation and explain why they chose the materials they did, the pattern they selected and why, and the overall concept illustrated.

3. Create an exhibit of tessellations in the room and organize a class digital portfolio of tessellations. Consider the following questions.
   a. What are the special challenges of creating tessellations?
   b. How effective are they as patterns for tessellations? Why do you think the Romans preferred them to other approaches to patterning?
   c. Create a blueprint for a mosaic floor in a Roman villa. How many tiles would be needed to create a complete floor in a room that measures 10 x 12 feet?

ASSESSMENT:

Assess tessellations with respect to creativity, accuracy, and organization. Blueprints should be assessed in respect to the model developed and the correctness of the problem solving.

LESSON 3

PROVERBS AND MOTTOS—A ROSE BY ANY OTHER NAME

Instructional Purpose: To study Latin proverbs and sayings that survive today.

Although we can study the vocabulary and grammar of Latin, it is also interesting to study the Latin words that are still used today to capture important ideas that we value in our culture. State mottos are one such form of Latin words that are used to represent important ideas. Proverbs, or adages, are another form that come to us directly from Roman authors. In this lesson, you will explore both mottos and proverbs and their meanings in English.

ACTIVITIES:

1. Ask students to examine the Latin mottos of five states. What do they mean in English? Comment on why they are appropriate for that state. (See Appendix B for the list.)

2. Now choose a new Latin motto for your state, based on recent history (last 20 years) and a review from the list of mottos in Appendix B. Develop an argument to have your new motto adopted for use in the state. Create an illustration to accompany the motto.

3. Share your new motto and illustration with the class. Articulate why it is superior to the current one in use.

4. Group students into pairs and have them select three proverbs from the list in Appendix C and study them with respect to the following aspects.
   a. What do they convey about Roman thought and belief?
   b. How are they similar and different from each other? Create a diagram to show the comparisons you made.
   c. How important are these ideas today? Where might we find them, although in other words?

5. Have students share their results from studying the proverbs. Discuss how proverbs were used in Rome and how they are used today.

6. Ask students to record in their journal an argument for the use of proverbs as a way to communicate *"multum in parvo."* Have them create a motto or proverb that best captures them at this stage of life and share selected ones in class.

ASSESSMENT:

Teachers may want to observe informally the work of the groups during this lesson to ensure depth of understanding of the written inscriptions.

LESSON 4

THE ROMAN HERO

Instructional Purpose: To understand the heroic cycle found in Roman and Greek myths.

The Olympian gods and goddesses preoccupied the thinking of the Romans to a great extent. However, they were also entranced with the heroes whose exploits were sung about and communicated across the ages. These heroes had godlike qualities but were mortal and often suffered for their deeds at the hands of jealous gods for their hubris or a fatal flaw that they possessed.

ACTIVITIES:

1. Ask students to read myths about these Greek and Roman heroes: Aeneas, Jason, Theseus, and Perseus.

2. Have students compete the chart below for two of the heroes cited, using the cycle of heroes model to describe the problem, the journey, the obstacles encountered, and the resolution. Students should analyze how the myths are similar yet different and answer these questions: Which hero is most effective in his mission(s)? Why do you think so?

	Problem	Journey	Obstacles	Resolution	Insights
Aeneas					
Jason					
Perseus					
Theseus					

3. Discuss the following questions as a class.
   a. What qualities did each hero have?
   b. What new insights did he gain from his adventures?
   c. How would you define a hero, based on your analysis of these four?

4. This unit is about the concept of expression. Have students use a chosen medium of expression to tell a story about a personal hero (or heroine) in their life. Use Handout 4.1: Writing a Myth as a guide.

RESOURCES FOR MYTHS:

Myths and legends (filmclips)—http://myths.e2bn.org/mythsandlegends

ASSESSMENT:

Students will be assessed on their myth project using the components of Handout 4.1: Writing a Myth.

HANDOUT 4.1

WRITING A MYTH

The components of a heroic myth

The hero—What qualities does your hero possess? What physical characteristics define him? Describe him in physical and moral ways.

The setting—Where does the myth take place? What are the characteristics of the landscape?

The journey—What happens in your myth? What journey does the hero take? What obstacles does he encounter? How do you resolve his journey?

The theme—What ideas does your myth convey about life and about your hero?

Respond to each of the questions above as you develop a draft of your story. Try to write the story of your hero within a 1,000 word limit (about 5 pages).

© Prufrock Press Inc. • *Ancient Roots and Ruins*

LESSON 5

ROMAN STATUARY

Instructional Purpose: To have students analyze and model the qualities of Roman statuary art.

The Romans were fond of statuary art to decorate their homes as well as their cities and temples. The art form often was realistic but also could be idealistic, conveying a virtue or quality of leadership that leaders wanted to convey to the people in the public context. Students will study selected pieces of statuary and create a composite model.

ACTIVITIES:

1. Have students study six pieces of Roman statuary found in the Metropolitan Museum of Art virtual tour (http://www.marchphoto.com/MetTour/index2.html). For the pieces they select, ask them to complete the following:
   a. What features do you see that are common across the statuary?
   b. What elements are distinctive?
   c. Write a description of each piece, based on what you see.
   d. Now draw a composite statue that incorporates different elements from each one.

2. Now ask students to discuss the Ruskin quote found at the beginning of Chapter 6:

   > Great nations write their autobiographies in three manuscripts, the book of their deeds, the book of their words, and the book of their art. Not one of these books can be understood unless we read the two others, but of the three, the only trustworthy one is the last.

3. Why is it important to understand the art of a culture? Discuss these ideas as a whole class.

4. Ask students to list the top three reasons and develop a written argument to support them. (This activity may be assigned as homework.) Discuss student arguments the next day.

LESSON 6

MYTH AS BELIEF

Instructional Purpose: To understand the role of myth in demonstrating religious belief.

Myths provided stories of how the world worked in many cultures, explaining the causes of human conflict, the reasons for natural disasters, and the patterns of daily life. The Romans, for example, viewed the stories of the gods and their exploits with humans as explanations for events that occurred and how men should live. These myths were passed down from generation to generation in poetry, prose, song, and oral discourse. Over time, artists reinterpreted stories from other ages and cultures in various ways, including music, painting, statuary, plays, and poetry.

ACTIVITIES:

1. Have students read one of the following myths:
   - Niobe and her daughters
   - Clytie
   - Narcissus
   - Arachne
   - Pyramus and Thisbe

2. Divide students into groups for discussing the following questions.
   a. What is the moral of the myth? What does it mean? Retitle it to reflect your understanding.
   b. Illustrate the myth by using symbols or icons to reflect the ideas. Articulate what your drawing conveys.
   c. What does the myth reveal about Roman philosophy or religious belief? How could you update the myth to reflect contemporary beliefs?
   d. Why did the Romans need myths? What purpose did they serve?

3. Have groups report their discussions to the class. Create a class comparison chart (see Handout 6.1) to reflect the similarities and differences noted among the myths selected for reading and analysis.

HANDOUT 6.1

MYTH COMPARISON CHART

Myth	Moral	Symbol	Belief	Purpose	Application Today

LESSON 7

ANIMALIA

Instructional Purpose: To represent realistic characteristics in a fantasy animal object à la the Romans.

Animals depicted in the art and mythology of the Romans are often combinations of several features of different animals such as the chimera (lion, snake, goat), the centaur (man and horse), the minotaur (man and bull), and the sphinx (woman and lion). These animal images dominate the myths and stories by providing concrete representations of qualities that were prized or feared. In this lesson, students will create their own mythological monster after studying ones commonly found in Rome.

ACTIVITIES:

1. Consult websites that depict these mythological creatures, such as Timeless Myths (http://www.timelessmyths.com/classical/beasts. html). What do you notice about the types of combinations used? Discuss as a class.
2. Ask students to create their own mythological animal with multiple characteristics, name the animal, and depict it in an art form of their choice. Share the resulting creatures in small groups.
3. Select six for whole-class sharing. Ask the student developers to present their creature and describe their thinking about the way they put characteristics together.

ASSESSMENT:

The animal products will be assessed according to the following criteria.

Organization	4	3	2	1
Representation of integrated traits	4	3	2	1
Creativity in representation	4	3	2	1
Articulation of thinking	4	3	2	1

LESSON 8

SYNTHESIS OF ART FORMS

Instructional Purpose: To demonstrate understanding of the connections between words and images in depicting a civilization.

The Romans expressed their ideas in words and images, many of which remain today in architectural structures, books, and artwork. These words and images represent the record we have of their civilization—artifacts we must interpret in their cultural context but also reinterpret in light of our current culture. In this lesson, students will have the opportunity to explore how words and images converge to create new levels of meaning that transcend time and space.

ACTIVITIES:

1. Have students create a montage of Roman words and images that illustrate well one of the following concepts central to their civilization:
   - time
   - power
   - duty
   - innovation

2. Students may present their montages and describe them using the following format.
   a. What idea did I select and why?
   b. What representations of the idea did I select?
   c. What is the connection between the words selected and the images?

3. Discuss the role of these concepts in understanding Roman civilization.

ASSESSMENT:

Montages will be assessed using the product rubric used in Lesson 7.

LESSON 9

VOCABULARY DEVELOPMENT

Instructional Purpose: To engage students in connecting English vocabulary to Latin roots and stems.

Ninety percent of English words that have three or more syllables come from Latin and/or Greek. Knowing Latin and Greek roots of words is a wonderful way for students to enhance their vocabulary. In this lesson, students will explore important terms studied in this unit and analyze their linguistic features.

ACTIVITIES:

1. Ask students to find the roots of the following words used in this unit, define them, and create at least 10 other words that use them in English (cognates). They should compose a paragraph that uses at least 5 of the original words or their cognates to reflect on their understanding of some aspect of Roman culture.
   a. philosophy
   b. mythology
   c. science
   d. metamorphosis
   e. aqueduct
   f. Pantheist
   g. expression

2. Ask students to share their paragraphs in small groups.
3. What were the favorite English words that students uncovered? Share and discuss.

LESSON 10

THE ROLE OF ORATORS IN ROMAN SOCIETY: BIOGRAPHY OF CICERO

Instructional Purpose: To explore the life and works of Cicero and a famous Roman of choice.

In this lesson, students will read about the most important orator in ancient Rome—Marcus Tullius Cicero.

ACTIVITIES:

1. Have students complete Handout 10.1: Biography Chart for Cicero and a famous Roman of their choosing, consulting the following websites.
   • Wikipedia (http://en.wikipedia.org/wiki)
   • Encyclopedia Brittanica (http://www.britannica.com/EBchecked/topic/117565/Marcus-Tullius-Cicero)
   • Open Library (http://www.openlibrary.org)

2. Ask the groups to report on key aspects of each life.
3. Ask students the following discussion questions.
   a. What aspect of Cicero's background indicated what role he might assume in Roman society?
   b. How did he prepare for his role in Roman society?
   c. What original contributions did each make?
   d. How important was oratory in Roman public life? Why?
   e. What have we learned from this ancient orator about the concept of expressions?

4. Have students write a 10-minute journal entry on the role of oral expression in our society. Who uses it and how? Toward what end? Share some examples and discuss.
5. Now ask students to read Handout 10.2: Cicero's Oration Against Catiline, one of the most famous from antiquity.

6. Ask students in small groups to identify the figures of speech he uses to heighten the dramatic effect of his oration. See Handout 10.3: Figures of Speech (Rhetorical Devices).

7. Have students prepare a short speech that uses at least three of these same figures of speech to argue for or against one of the following:
   a. gun control in the U.S.
   b. affirmative action
   c. wealth redistribution via higher taxes on the wealthy

8. Ask three students to share their speeches and have the class identify the rhetorical devices used.

9. Have students do a biography project on a famous Roman. Pass out page 229.

STUDENT BIOGRAPHY PROJECT ON A FAMOUS ROMAN

Each of you will select a famous Roman—Cato, Catullus, Ovid, Plautus, or Pompey—to study as a part of this unit. You will prepare a Biography Chart on the person you select and use it as the basis for your written report (3–5 pages) and presentation (5 minutes). The biography report and presentation must address the following components:

- Introduce and explain who this famous Roman is by selecting 7–10 interesting points about his life that relate to the elements studied in the biographical chart you prepared.
- Describe in your own words what you think this person's lasting impact and contributions are to the field or domain in which they operate.
- Explain the most important thing you learned about the concept of innovation/expression by reading about the life of this person and identify any new insights that you uncovered as a result of your work.

HANDOUT 10.1

BIOGRAPHY CHART

Name of person:_____

Birth date and death date:_____

Family members (at birth):_____

Extended family (e.g., spouse, children): _____

Early education/continued education:_____

Interests and predispositions:_____

_____

Personality characteristics: _____

_____

Abilities:_____

_____

Role he or she played in Roman history:_____

_____

_____

Contributions:_____

Important quotes (3–5):_____

_____

_____

Awards and honors:_____

Is your person an innovator or creator? Explain. _____

Why is he or she still remembered today?_____

_____

_____

© Prufrock Press Inc. • *Ancient Roots and Ruins*

HANDOUT 10.2

CICERO'S ORATION AGAINST CATILINE

Marcus Tullius Cicero (Cicero)
1st Catilinarian Oration (In Catilinam)

O tempora, o mores! Senatus haec intellegit. Consul videt; hic tamen vivit. Vivit? immo vero etiam in senatum venit, fit publici consilii particeps, notat et designat oculis ad caedem unum quemque nostrum. Nos autem fortes viri satisfacere rei publicae videmur, si istius furorem ac tela vitemus. Ad mortem te, Catilina, duci iussu consulis iam pridem oportebat, in te conferri pestem, quam tu in nos [omnes iam diu] machinaris.

An vero vir amplissumus, P. Scipio, pontifex maximus, Ti. Gracchum mediocriter labefactantem statum rei publicae privatus interfecit; Catilinam orbem terrae caede atque incendiis vastare cupientem nos consules perferemus? Nam illa nimis antiqua praetereo, quod C. Servilius Ahala Sp. Maelium novis rebus studentem manu sua occidit. Fuit, fuit ista quondam in hac re publica virtus, ut viri fortes acrioribus suppliciis civem perniciosum quam acerbissimum hostem coercerent. Habemus senatus consultum in te, Catilina, vehemens et grave, non deest rei publicae consilium neque auctoritas huius ordinis; nos, nos, dico aperte, consules desumus.

Shame on the age and on its principles! The senate is aware of these things; the consul sees them; and yet this man lives. Lives! aye, he comes even into the senate. He takes a part in the public deliberations; he is watching and marking down and checking off for slaughter every individual among us. And we, gallant men that we are, think that we are doing our duty to the republic if we keep out of the way of his frenzied attacks. You ought, O Catiline, long ago to have been led to execution by command of the consul. That destruction which you have been long plotting against us ought to have already fallen on your own head.

What? Did not that most illustrious man, Publius Scipio, the Pontifex Maximus, in his capacity of a private citizen, put to death Tiberius Gracchus, though but slightly undermining the constitution? And shall we, who are the consuls, tolerate Catiline, openly desirous to destroy the whole world with fire and slaughter? For I pass over older instances, such as how Caius Servilius Ahala with his own hand slew Spurius Maelius when plotting a revolution in the state. There was—there was once such virtue in this republic, that brave men would repress mischievous citizens with severer chastisement than the most bitter enemy. For we have a resolution of the senate, a formidable and authoritative decree against you, O Catiline; the wisdom of the republic is not at fault, nor the dignity of this senatorial body. We, we alone,—I say it openly, —we, the consuls, are waiting in our duty.

Translated by C.D. Yonge

HANDOUT 10.3
FIGURES OF SPEECH
(RHETORICAL DEVICES)

Alliteration: repetition of the same consonant at the beginning of successive words (e.g., *magno murmure montis*—*The Aeneid*)

Anaphora: repetition of the same word at the beginning of successive clauses (e.g., "<u>love</u> led me here, <u>love</u> told me what to do, <u>love</u> drove my life")

Antithesis: expression of two contrasting elements or opinions, side by side (e.g., *Odi et amo*, I hate and I love—Catullus)

Apostrophe: an address directed to an abstract concept or a representation of an abstract concept (e.g., "Oh fates, why do you toy with us?")

Hyperbole: the use of exaggeration for effect (e.g., "I ran a million miles today")

Irony: a statement that expresses a difference between the literal and implied meaning (e.g., "But Brutus says he was ambitious and Brutus is an honorable man" —Shakespeare's *Julius Caesar*)

Metaphor: a method of describing an object as if it were another unlike object (e.g., "the boat slithered on the water like a snake")

Metonymy: the use of a symbol to stand for an idea or object (e.g., using the word "crown" as a stand-in for "king")

Onomatopoeia: the use of words that sound like the word they mean (e.g., "squelch"; "ululate," meaning "it shrieks" in Latin)

Oxymoron: an expression of two apparently opposite concepts (e.g., *festina lente*, meaning "make haste slowly" in Latin)

Personification: the attribution of human qualities to an abstract concept or an object (e.g., "when life hands you lemons, you'll understand personification")

Simile: a method of describing an object as if it were another unlike object, using the word "like" or "as" (e.g., "the boat slithered on the water like a snake")

© Prufrock Press Inc. • *Ancient Roots and Ruins*

UNIT ASSESSMENT

Allow one period of 40 minutes for the essay activity to be completed. Give students the following prompt:

- Develop an argument that contends the following: Roman culture provides important insights into our own.
- Be sure to state your opinion, support it with at least three examples that you elaborate on, and include a conclusion.

The rubric to be used for assessing the unit essay may be found in Handout 6.3: Persuasive Writing Rubric.

UNIT 6

ROMAN LEGACY

> *Nescire autem quid ante quam natus sis*
> *acciderit, id est semper esse puerum.*
> Not to know what happened before you
> were born is to be a child forever.
>
> —Cicero's *Letters*

KEY GENERALIZATIONS

» Legacies provide evidence of the nature, scope, and value of an enterprise.
» Legacies demonstrate both the universal and enduring value of human activity.
» Legacies may be transferred directly or be modified in their translation to other contexts.

ESSENTIAL QUESTIONS

» How do the concepts fit together?

In this unit, students will explore the connections between the concepts they have studied: expression, innovation, time, space, and power. They will create a concept map that shows their understanding of the interrelationships of the concepts and their underlying topics that have been studied. They will use these concept maps to present their synthesized understanding of Roman culture and civilization.

» Why was Rome a great civilization?

As students have studied various aspects of Roman culture and language, they have come to see the nature and extent of Rome's influence on the ancient world. This influence extended well beyond the boundaries of Italy, Gaul, and Ionia and came to influence the known Western world at the time. The students will be able to identify and describe the most remarkable achievements of this culture that have survived the test of time and influence in contemporary society.

» Why did Rome decline?

It took hundreds of years for Rome and its mighty empire to collapse. However, many factors contributed to its decline and loss of power. Students will be able to analyze the factors that contributed to this circumstance in the history of the world. They can also compare how these factors have impacted other cultures in similar ways. They can also analyze their own culture in respect to these factors and consider whether America is in a state of decline or not.

GOALS AND OUTCOMES

» Develop a connected understanding of the core concepts studied to Roman civilization.

Students will be able to:
- create a concept map for each concept studied, and
- develop overall generalizations about Roman civilization.

» Develop an appreciation for the legacy of Roman civilization.

Students will be able to:
- demonstrate understanding of legacy areas that the Roman civilization has bequeathed, and
- research one area in which Roman civilization has impacted across time and culture.

» Analyze the development and decline of Roman civilization.

Students will be able to:
- evaluate factors that contributed to development and those that contributed to the decline of Roman civilization, and
- create an argument for the causes of Rome's decline.

LESSON 1

CONCEPT MAPS (3 PERIODS)

Instructional Purpose: To demonstrate the interconnectedness of the topics studied about Roman language and civilization.

ACTIVITIES:

1. Ask students in small groups to create concept maps addressing one of the overarching concepts studied in the five units on Roman civilization—time, space, power, innovation, and expression. What are examples of the concept generalizations? How does the concept work in respect to Roman civilization?
2. Provide Handout 1.1: Concept Map for each group to work from. Score using Rubric 2: Scoring Rubric for Concept Maps.

PART I

Students should create concept maps that will be assessed on three aspects: the hierarchal level where students move from the abstract to the concrete in respect to specific examples, the propositions where students establish links across concepts, and the example level where students provide concrete examples of a concept.

Sample concept: Power
*   Includes types of power such as persuasive, role designation, economic, and military
*   Uses of power such as expansion of territory, building of reputation as a leader, and spreading worldview to other cultures
*   Outcomes of power such as growth of civilization, decay of civilization, and great cultural artifacts
*   Traits of powerful people such as military glory, money, oratorical skill, and writing skill
*   Symbols of power such as monuments, busts and statues, patronage, and inscriptions

PART II

Student groups create unit concept maps from which a large concept map and generalizations about Roman civilization are drawn. Sample generalizations that the class may consider might be:

- Roman civilization influenced the development of Western cultures, including our own.
- Roman civilization impacted most significantly in the spheres of language, government, law, medicine, and the arts.
- Roman civilization contributed important applications of concepts about how the world works (e.g., time, space, power).
- Roman civilization integrated new ideas and technologies from other cultures to create lasting contributions (e.g., the arch, *The Aeneid*)

3. Have each group report via chart paper on the wall or on a visualizer. Ask each group to justify their examples and choices.
4. Compare the five resulting concept maps with each other in respect to overlaps, discrepancies, and connections. Discuss these areas and make revisions as appropriate.
5. Create a set of generalizations about Roman civilization based on the concept map activity. What ideas transcend the individual concepts studied?
6. Present each of the generalizations as a claim for Roman civilization, providing multiple forms of evidence to support each claim.
7. Close the class discussion with this question: What are the most important ideas we have come to understand about Roman civilization?

NAME:_____ DATE:_____

HANDOUT 1.1

CONCEPT MAP

Concepts Studied	Generalizations	Applications
Time		
Space		
Power		
Innovation		
Expression		

© Prufrock Press Inc. • *Ancient Roots and Ruins*

RUBRIC 2: SCORING RUBRIC FOR CONCEPT MAPS

Directions for Use: Score students on their completed maps.

	5	4	3	2	1	0
Hierarchical Level Each subordinate concept is more specific and less general than the concept drawn above it. Count the number of levels included in the total map.	Five or more levels are identified.	Four levels are identified.	Three levels are identified.	Two levels are identified.	One level is identified.	No hierarchical levels are identified.
Propositions The linking of two concepts indicating a clear relationship is given. Count the total number of propositions identified on the total map.	Twelve or more propositions are provided.	Ten to twelve propositions are provided.	Seven to nine propositions are provided.	Four to six propositions are provided.	One to three propositions are provided.	No propositions are provided.
Examples A valid example of a concept is provided. Count the total number of examples.	Twelve or more examples are provided.	Ten to twelve examples are provided.	Seven to nine examples are provided.	Four to six examples are provided.	One to three examples are provided.	No examples are provided.

Total points possible: 15

LESSON 2

LEGACY ANALYSIS

Instructional Purpose: To evaluate the achievements of ancient Rome in respect to their contemporary importance.

ACTIVITIES:

1. Ask students in small groups to review the following 10 areas of contribution by the Romans, studied in the units:
   - myth and literature
   - governmental structures
   - military tactics
   - measurement of time
   - architecture (housing—mosaics and wall painting)
   - engineering technology (bridges and arches)
   - language (alphabet, roots, stems, vocabulary, and grammatical structures)
   - mottos, proverbs, and idioms
   - eminent people
   - astronomy and astrology

2. Based on this list, students should analyze the current impact of the ideas on our beliefs, values, and practices today in the United States. They can use Handout 2.1: Contemporary Analysis of Roman Contributions as the organizer for recording their ideas. Have them share in groups.

3. Now have each student select one legacy area of interest and locate evidence to support its importance in the world today. They should create a poster, persuasive essay, film, or collage to display their results.

4. Have students present their legacy arguments to the class. Encourage questions and answers. Engage students in peer assessment.

5. Based on peer ratings, the top five legacy projects will be shared in a public forum.

ASSESSMENT:

Students will be judged on their legacy projects according to the following criteria and scale (4 being excellent, 3 being good, 2 being fair, and 1 being poor):

Use of examples	4	3	2	1
Creative integration of ideas	4	3	2	1
Evidence of content understanding	4	3	2	1
Effective use of form (i.e., essay, poster, film, or collage)	4	3	2	1
Clarity of presentation	4	3	2	1
Organization of the product	4	3	2	1
Strengths of the product:				
Areas for improvement:				

This form should be used as both a peer assessment and teacher assessment.

HANDOUT 2.1
CONTEMPORARY ANALYSIS OF ROMAN CONTRIBUTIONS

myth and literature

governmental structures

military tactics

measurement of time

architecture (housing—mosaics and wall painting)

© Prufrock Press Inc. • *Ancient Roots and Ruins*

HANDOUT 2.1, CONTINUED

engineering technology (bridges and arches)

language (alphabet, roots, stems, vocabulary, and grammatical structures)

mottos, proverbs, and idioms

eminent people

astronomy and astrology

LESSON 3

DECLINE AND FALL FROM GREATNESS: LESSONS LEARNED

> The barbarians are the brooms which sweep the
> historical stage clear of the debris of a dead civilization;
> this destructive feat is their historic task . . .
> —Arnold Toynbee

Instructional Purpose: To analyze and evaluate the trends toward decline in the Roman Empire.

ACTIVITIES:

1. Ask students to consider the following factors that have been discussed in the preceding units and may have accounted for the fall of the Roman Empire:
   - the overextension of resources to fight foreign wars
   - heavy taxation of citizens
   - the persistent invasion of barbarian tribes
   - periods of stagnation and corrupt leadership
   - internal conflicts and excesses of the Roman people

2. Have students read *The Hunger Games* by Suzanne Collins. Discuss the following questions:
   a. The nation of Panem is described in *The Hunger Games* as having similar factors to those affecting Rome in its period of decline. Cite what those factors are and the support for them in the text.
   b. The primary character of Katniss Everdeen was modeled on the Roman slave-turned-gladiator Spartacus. What rebellious acts does she commit that threaten Panem?
   c. How do the people of Panem ultimately cause the collapse of the nation? Consider the factors of leadership, internal conflict, and external strife.

3. After considering the factors for Rome's decline listed earlier and using the analogy of *The Hunger Games*, discuss in pairs the evidence to support each of the factors listed and rate them from high to low in respect to importance.

4. Now read selections from contemporary historians (e.g., Adrian Goldsworthy) regarding the fall of Rome. What perspectives do they have that are different from your conclusions? Would they rate the factors in the same way? Why or why not?

ASSESSMENT:

Conclude the lesson by having students write a persuasive essay for 40 minutes on what accounted for the fall of Rome. Use the rubric found in Handout 3.1: Persuasive Writing Rubric to assess the essays.

NAME: _____ DATE: _____

HANDOUT 3.1

PERSUASIVE WRITING RUBRIC

	0	2	4	6	8
Claim or Opinion	No clear position exists on the writer's assertion, preference, or view, and context does not help to clarify it.	Yes/no alone or writer's position is poorly formulated, but reader is reasonably sure what the paper is about based on context.	A clear topic sentence exists, and the reader is reasonably sure what the paper is about based on the strength of the topic sentence alone.	A very clear, concise position is given and position is elaborated with reference to reasons; multiple sentences are used to form the claim. Must include details that explain the context.	n/a
Data or Supporting Point	No reasons are offered that are relevant to the claim.	One or two weak reasons are offered; the reasons are relevant to the claim.	At least two strong reasons are offered that are relevant to the claim.	At least three reasons are offered that are relevant to the claim.	At least three reasons are offered that are also accurate, convincing, and distinct.
Elaboration	No elaboration is provided.	An attempt is made to elaborate at least one reason.	More than one reason is supported with relevant details.	Each reason (three) is supported with relevant information that is clearly connected to the claim.	The writer explains all reasons in a very effective, convincing, multiparagraph structure.
Conclusion	No conclusion/ closing sentence is provided.	A conclusion/ closing sentence is provided.	A conclusion is provided that revisits the main ideas.	A strong concluding paragraph is provided that revisits and summarizes main ideas.	n/a

248

APPENDIX A

PRONUNCIATION AND NUMBER GUIDE

There are two major systems of pronunciation in Latin: classical and ecclesiastical. Ecclesiastical pronunciation is primarily used by the Catholic Church, and came into use after the traditional date of the fall of Rome (476 CE). This pronunciation guide will help you with the more ancient pronunciation, known as Classical Latin.

The Latin alphabet is very similar to our own, but the letters "w" and "j" do not exist in Classical Latin. Follow the chart below and practice the sounds.

Consonants

c	Always a hard consonant, like a "k" (e.g., c as in "cat")
g	Always a hard consonant (e.g., g as in "game")
i	Before another vowel, this is pronounced like a "y" (e.g., "ianua," meaning door, is pronounced "ya-new-ah")
r	Rolled sound (e.g., the first r in "sombrero")
s	Always soft, never like a "z" (e.g., s as in "same")
v	Always makes a "w" sound (e.g., "villa," meaning country home, is pronounced "will-ah")

Vowels

- In Latin, some vowels have a macron (or long mark) over them like this: amīca, sedēre, fūgiō
- When this happens, the vowel is long, and should be held about twice as long as a short vowel.

Vowel Short Long

a	=	"almond"
e	=	"get"
i	=	"rip"
o	=	"more"
u	=	"foot"

ā	=	"father"
ē	=	"late"
ī	=	"meet"
ō	=	"whole"
ū	=	"root"

In Latin there are also certain diphthongs to know—a diphthong is two vowels next to each other that make one sound—there are two important ones to know, listed below.

- ae = pronounced as the word eye (e.g., *villae* meaning country houses)
- au = pronounced as the "ow" in the word "how" (e.g., *aurum* meaning gold)

The last rule of Latin pronunciation to remember is that every vowel represents one syllable, with the exception of the diphthongs listed above, so a word like *religione* is pronounced "re-li-gi-o-ne."

Number Guide

Number	Numeral	Latin Number
1	I	Ūnus, Ūna, Ūnum
2	II	Duo, Duae, Dua
3	III	Trēs, Trēs, Tria
4	IV	Quattuor
5	V	Quinque
6	VI	Sex
7	VII	Septem
8	VIII	Octo
9	IX	Novem
10	X	Decem

Number	Numeral	Latin Number
11	XI	Undecim
12	XII	Duodecim
13	XIII	Trēdecim
14	XIV	Quattuordecim
15	XV	Quindecim
16	XVI	Sēdecim
17	XVII	Septendecim
18	XVIII	Duodēviginti
19	XIX	Undēviginti
20	XX	Viginti
50	L	Quinquaginta
100	C	Centum
1000	M	Mille

APPENDIX B

STATE MOTTOS

State	Latin Motto	English Translation
Alabama	*Audemus jura nostra defendere*	We dare defend our rights
Arizona	*Ditat Deus*	God enriches
Arkansas	*Regnat populus*	The people rule
Colorado	*Nil sine numine*	Nothing without the deity
Connecticut	*Qui transtulit sustinet*	He who transplanted sustains
District of Columbia	*Justitia Omnibus*	Justice for All
Idaho	*Esto perpetua*	Let it be perpetual
Kansas	*Ad astra per aspera*	To the stars through difficulties
Kentucky	*Deo gratiam habeamus*	Let us be grateful to God
Maine	*Dirigo*	I lead
Massachusetts	*Ense petit placidam sub libertate quietem*	By the sword we seek peace, but peace only under liberty
Michigan	*Si quaeris peninsulam amoenam circumspice*	If you seek a pleasant peninsula, look about you
Mississippi	*Virtute et armis*	By valor and arms
Missouri	*Salus populi suprema lex esto*	Let the welfare of the people be the supreme law
New Mexico	*Crescit eundo*	It grows as it goes
New York	*Excelsior*	Ever upward
North Carolina	*Esse quam videri*	To be, rather than to seem

State	Latin Motto	English Translation
North Dakota	*Serit ut alteri saeclo prosit*	One sows for the benefit of another age
Oklahoma	*Labor omnia vincit*	Work conquers all things
Oregon	*Alis volat propriis*	She flies with her own wings
South Carolina	*Dum spiro spero*	While I breathe, I hope
South Carolina	*Animis opibusque parati*	Ready in soul and resource
Virginia	*Sic semper tyrannis*	Thus always to tyrants
West Virginia	*Montani semper liberi*	Mountaineers are always free

APPENDIX C

LIST OF LATIN PROVERBS, IDIOMS, AND COMMON PHRASES

> *Carpe diem, quam minimum credula postero.*
> Seize the day, trust as little as possible in tomorrow.
>
> —Horace

- *Concordia res parvae crescent.* Work together to accomplish more.
- *Credula vitam spes fovet et melius cras fore semper dicit.* (Credulous) hope supports our life, and always says that tomorrow will be better. (Tibullus)
- *Est modus in rebus.* There is a middle ground in things. (Horace)
- *Forsan haec et olim meminisse iuvabit.* Perhaps one day it will help to remember even these things. (Vergil, *The Aeneid*)
- *Homo vitae commodatus non donatus est.* Man has been lent to life, not given. (Pubilius Syrus)
- *Horas non numero nisi serenas.* I count only the bright hours. (Inscription on ancient sundials)
- *Inventas vitam iuvat excoluisse per artes.* Let us improve life through the arts. (Vergil)
- *Ipsa quidem pretium virtus sibi.* Virtue is its own reward.

255

- *Ipsa scientia potestas est.* Knowledge itself is power. (Francis Bacon)
- *Legum servi sumus ut liberi esse possimus.* We are slaves of the law so that we may be able to be free. (Cicero)
- *Leve fit, quod bene fertur, onus.* The burden is made light which is borne well. (Ovid)
- *Magister artis ingeniique largitor venter.* Necessity is the mother of all invention. (Aesop)
- *Magna res est vocis et silentii temperamentum.* The great thing is to know when to speak and when to keep quiet.
- *Manus manum lavat.* One hand washes the other. (Petronius)
- *Materiam superabat opus.* The workmanship was better than the subject matter. (Ovid)
- *Mens sana in corpore sano.* A sound mind in a sound body. (Juvenal)
- *Multi famam, conscientiam pauci verentur.* Many fear their reputation, few their conscience. (Pliny)
- *Multi sunt vocati, pauci vero electi.* Many are called [but] few are chosen.
- *Non omne quod nitet aurum est.* Not all that glitters is gold.
- *Non scholae sed vitae discimus.* We do not learn for school, but for life. (Seneca)
- *Nulla avarita sine poena est.* There is no avarice without penalty. (Seneca)
- *Nulla dies sine linea.* Not a day without a line. Do something every day! (Apeles, Greek painter)
- *Omnia mea mecum porto.* All that is mine, I carry with me. (My wisdom is my greatest wealth; Cicero)
- *Astra inclinant, non necessitant.* The stars incline; they do not determine.
- *Aurea mediocrita.* The golden mean. (An ethical goal; truth and goodness are generally to be found in the middle; Horace)
- *Aut viam inveniam aut faciam.* I will either find a way or make one.
- *Ave atque vale.* Hail and farewell. (Catullus)

COMMON PHRASES IN ENGLISH DERIVED FROM LATIN

ad infinitum—to the eternal, to go on and on

ante bellum—before the war

bona fide—in good faith

ex post facto—after the fact

ex libris—from the books

in absentia—in absence

in loco parentis—in the place of parents; acting as a guardian

in medias res—in the middle of things

in memoriam—in memory of

in re—in the case of

ipso facto—by the fact itself

multum in parvo—much in a small amount; less is more

per annum—per year

per diem—by the day

per se—by oneself; essentially

post mortem—after death

quid pro quo—something for something; an even exchange

sine qua non—a necessity

status quo—the existing condition

terra firma—solid ground

verbatim—word for word

vice versa—turned the other way

ABOUT THE AUTHORS

Ariel Baska teaches all levels of Latin in Fairfax County Public Schools. She received her bachelor's degree in classics from The College of William and Mary and her master's degree in curriculum studies with an emphasis in gifted education at George Mason University. She has presented at large foreign language and gifted education conferences, including the National Association for Gifted Children, the Asia-Pacific Conference on Giftedness, and the World Conference for Gifted and Talented. She has written two Navigators (curriculum related to the teaching of literature) with the Center for Gifted Education at William and Mary—one for John Steinbeck's *The Pearl* and one for Shakespeare's *Twelfth Night*. She cowrote an article in the *Gifted Education Communicator* titled "*Working With Gifted Students With Special Needs*." She also cowrote a chapter on the role of the arts in the affective development of the gifted in *Social and Emotional Curriculum for Gifted Students* (2008). To contribute to her mother's Festschrift, she wrote a chapter on the educational contributions of Sir Francis Galton in *Leading Change* (2010).

Joyce VanTassel-Baska is Professor Emerita at The College of William and Mary, where she founded the Center for Gifted Education. Formerly she initiated and directed the Center for Talent Development at Northwestern University. Joyce has also served as state director of gifted

259

programs in Illinois, a regional director, a local coordinator of gifted programs, and a teacher of gifted high school students. Her major research interests are in the talent development process and effective curricular interventions with the gifted.

She is the author of 22 books and has written more than 500 other publications on gifted education. She was the editor of *Gifted and Talented International* for several years and received the Distinguished Scholar Award in 1997 from the National Association for Gifted Children and the Outstanding Faculty Award from the State Council of Higher Education in Virginia in 1993. She received the Distinguished Alumna Achievement Award from the University of Toledo in 2003, the President's Award from the World Council on Gifted and Talented in 2005, and the Collaboration and Diversity Service Award from CEC-TAG in 2007.